AUTHENTIC ITALIAN

A FEAST OF ITALIAN RECIPES FROM THE VINCENZO'S PLATE FAMILY

VINCENZO & SUZANNE PROSPERI

8	**BENVENUTI**
18	**ANTIPASTI**
56	**SAUCES**
76	**FRESH PASTA**
96	**PRIMI (BUT MOSTLY PASTA)**
160	**PIZZA E PANE**
182	**SECONDI**
208	**DOLCI**
230	**INDEX**
238	**GRAZIE**

IT ALL STARTED WITH LOVE ...

More than a decade of carefully and meticulously building an online Italian foodie community, and here we are, at one of the greatest milestones we could ever have dreamed of: our very own cookbook. Along the way, we've grown an online family of millions globally, welcomed two beautiful babies, plus hosted some of the most spectacular Italian-themed events imaginable. Not to mention dabbled in private catering, hosted cooking classes for all ages, and created annual sold-out tours of Vincenzo's home-region of Abruzzo in Italy (something so close to our hearts that we often refer to it as our first baby, but officially named Italy Unexplored).

What started as love at first sight – a romance between a handsome young Italian tourist visiting Australia and a third-generation Calabrese Italian, born and raised in the land Down Under – has transformed into an epic adventure building the Vincenzo's Plate family, as well as our very own!

OUR INSPIRATION

Vincenzo has always had a love for entertaining and eating, and we have always been passionate about our culture and its incredible food, so once we put Vincenzo in front of the camera, there was no holding us back.

It all started with recreating classic recipes and our family favourites. Before we knew it, we were filling our days filming recipes we've been eating since we were young, sharing authentic cuisine, from Abruzzo and Calabria in particular, with the world. Many dishes are odes to those recipes Vincenzo was taught during his time working in restaurants globally, and others are from family and friends who have shared their treasured dishes with us over the years. Many of these recipes – and life lessons – come from Vincenzo's grandmother, Nonna Igea, who is now well into her eighties, and who was already cooking for her village when she was 12.

Vincenzo's passion for food also started early. Growing up surrounded by his *nonni* and *bisnonni* (grandparents and great-grandparents), he spent countless hours in their kitchens and gardens, watching, learning, tasting and, almost unknowingly, being inspired. His family's traditions, stories and unwavering dedication to fresh, quality ingredients planted the seed for his love of cooking. These moments shaped not only his palate but also his deep respect for keeping things simple and allowing the ingredients to shine, and formed the foundation of his mantra that 'food brings people together'.

Suzanne grew up just a few streets away from her nonni in suburban Sydney, and her mornings often began with the scents of the fresh ricotta or homegrown vegetables that her nonno (also named Vincenzo) would deliver to her door bright and early. Her nonni never missed an opportunity to share their love through food, arriving at all of her family's birthdays and events with boxes (literally, boxes – huge ones) of homemade biscuits, always ready to feed family and friends.

OUR REASON AND 'THE FEELING'

It could be said that the generosity of our nonni's generation is unmatched – and perhaps it's not just their recipes that have been lost over time. The feeling they created, the meaning in all that they did, ignites a fire in us every single day, to ensure their memories live on, not just in the food they prepared but also in the ways they made us feel and the importance they placed on being together.

This book is bursting with recipe ideas to ignite your passion for cooking, as well as a sprinkle of family stories in between. We could have written for months and still not had enough pages – the hardest part of writing this book was choosing which recipes to leave out!

As we continue to open our hearts – and our kitchen – to your families, our hope is that this book becomes a little Italian cooking bible for you. May it be cherished for generations, with recipes recreated with love for family, friends and even for only yourselves, on grand occasions or simply just because.

SHARING OUR STORY

As you flip through the pages, we hope you'll be transported to Italy, imagining the aromas soon to be filling your home. Every recipe includes Suzanne's memories of the dish, as well as Vincenzo's flair and invaluable tips. In sharing these stories, we aim to remind you – as we are reminded every day – that family is at the heart of everything we do.

Where a recipe comes from one of our inspirations, be it Nonna Igea, a family member or a foodie friend, we

have included their tips to ensure you have support from them as you recreate their dishes.

Creating this book has been to open our kitchens to you, and we have done so with an immense amount of gratitude for the opportunity. Our mission is simple: to empower you to cook the most authentic and scrumptious Italian dishes in your own kitchens, using fresh, quality ingredients, to create magic in every bite.

QUALITY INGREDIENTS

Italian cooking is, at its heart, about celebrating high-quality, fresh ingredients and letting them shine. This timeless philosophy has been lovingly passed down through generations, and it's one we hold close in everything we create. Every ingredient has its own story, and when you choose the best, you allow those stories to unfold on the plate – simple, honest, and full of flavour.

The Mediterranean diet is a beautiful example of this approach. It's built on wholesome ingredients – think vibrant vegetables, fresh seafood, whole grains, nuts and, of course, extra virgin olive oil. This isn't just a way of eating; it's a way of life. And one of the simplest yet most striking examples of letting quality, fresh, seasonal produce shine is the classic Insalata Caprese (see recipe, page 22).

Vincenzo always marvels at how some people will pay exorbitant prices to dine out on a simple plate of pasta or bruschetta (though let's be honest, we love a good night out too), but then hesitate to spend just a few extra dollars on quality ingredients to cook at home. It's not about being extravagant – it's about making choices that elevate the everyday. Why settle for less when the best is within reach? A better brand of pasta, rich peeled tomatoes, or the freshest vegetables can make all the difference and feed your family with love and authenticity. Plus, when you make dishes at home, you'll often have leftovers, so in the end, the cost per meal is far less.

Meals are like a celebration of what's fresh, seasonal and nourishing, proving that good food doesn't need to be complicated to be extraordinary. When you focus on quality and let the ingredients do the talking, you'll find yourself cooking with more confidence, more joy and more connection to the people you share your table with. That's the true essence of Italian cooking, and our number-one hope for how this book might inspire you in your home.

VINCENZO'S GOLDEN RULES OF ITALIAN COOKING

HOW TO BUY DRY PACKED PASTA

Not all pasta is created equal, and when you go to the supermarket or your local grocer, you should be aware of what to look for, because it makes a world of difference.

Always choose pasta made with 100 per cent durum wheat (*semola di grano duro*) – this is the foundation for the perfect texture. There should be very few ingredients in the dry pasta – water and semolina are all that's needed.

Look out for messaging such as 'pasta trafilata al bronzo', which means it is shaped the traditional way, giving it a rough surface perfect for soaking up all the delicious flavours of your sauce. Like I always say, 'Your ingredients need to make love!'

Good-quality pasta should be light yellow in colour. If it looks more orange, it's probably not the best choice – the colour is a sign of the drying process, which means the pasta was dried at a lower temperature for a longer time.

THE ALL-IMPORTANT SOFFRITTO

Soffritto (meaning 'sautéed' or 'fried gently' in Italian) is the key to many classic Italian dishes. It's a simple mix of finely chopped onions, carrots and celery, sautéed in extra virgin olive oil to create a base. While some Italians skip it in their sauces, it's a staple in my home region of Abruzzo, and I can't imagine my Tomato and basil sugo (see recipe, page 60) without it. I chop all the veggies roughly then add them to a blender with extra virgin olive oil before letting it simmer in the pan, because I find this really infuses the sauce with the added flavours. The way the carrot gently sweetens the sauce is why I never skip soffritto – if you've never tried it, do yourself a favour and add it to your basic sauce recipe. It's amazing how much flavour it adds!

LIQUID GOLD
(AKA EXTRA VIRGIN OLIVE OIL)

Extra virgin olive oil (EVOO) is an essential ingredient in many Italian dishes. It balances flavours, adds depth, and even boasts nutritional benefits. But not all EVOO is the same, so choosing the right one is crucial.

Here are my top tips for finding the best liquid gold for your kitchen.

READ THE LABEL

Check where the olives come from. The best EVOO often hails from Italy, Greece or Spain, but don't be fooled by labels that say it was simply 'packed' there. Always look for 'single-origin' olives, which means all the olives used come from one location. Avoid vague mention of 'imported ingredients', which usually indicates a blend of lower-quality olives.

GO COLD PRESSED ONLY

Authentic, quality EVOO must be cold pressed – a process that ensures the oil is never heated above 27°C (86°F) and uses no chemicals. Cold pressing preserves the natural flavours and nutrients of the olives, making it the gold standard for premium olive oil. Anything less just isn't worth it.

TASTE TEST LIKE A PRO

If you're lucky enough to sample before you buy, here's how to do it right. Pour a little EVOO into a glass and warm it by cupping the bottom of the glass in your hand, twisting your palm back and forth. Next, take a deep sniff with both nostrils and then sip a small amount. Swirl it around your palate, raise your tongue to the roof of your mouth, and breathe in lightly to let the oil trickle down your throat. Pay attention to the flavours – it might feel robust and spicy, or even mild and grassy. A tickle at the back of your throat is usually a sign of high quality. If sampling multiple oils, cleanse your palate with water and a bite of apple between tastings.

FORGET THE COLOUR

Don't judge an EVOO by its shade. Colour varies by olive variety and the freshness of the press, so it's not a reliable indicator of quality.

CHECK THE DATE

EVOO is best consumed within 12 months of harvesting, for peak flavour. It's still safe after that, but its flavours and intensity will fade.

THE ITALIAN STAPLES WE CAN'T LIVE WITHOUT

While an exhaustive list might be too long for this book, these are the things we always have on hand at home. They're a combination of store-bought and homemade.

PANTRY
- canned peeled Italian tomatoes
- passata (see recipe, page 74)
- dry active yeast
- dried (quality) pasta, all our favourite shapes
- carnaroli and arborio rice
- canned legumes: lentils, chickpeas and cannellini beans are favourites
- almonds, pine nuts and pistachios
- breadcrumbs (see tips, page 146, to make your own)
- dried oregano
- peperoncino (chilli pepper)
- whole or ground nutmeg
- plain (all-purpose) flour
- tipo '00' flour
- extra virgin olive oil (of course)
- rock salt

FRESH
- basil
- eggs
- onions
- garlic
- carrots
- celery
- in-season fruits and vegetables

FRIDGE/FREEZER
- Pecorino Romano (Don't question it – if you know me, you know!)
- Parmigiano Reggiano (and leftover rinds)
- full-cream milk
- ricotta
- pesto (see recipe, page 64)
- salami
- guanciale
- portions of leftover Sugo and Bolognese ragù (see recipes, pages 60 and 63)

FRESH vs DRIED HERBS

Both work in Italian cooking; it really depends on the dish. I love using fresh herbs like parsley, basil and thyme to finish a dish, adding them at the end to maximise their flavour infusion. Dried herbs, on the other hand, such as oregano, sage and rosemary, are perfect for slow-cooked dishes like porchetta and minestrone.

BASIL RULES

The golden rule for basil, one of the most common herbs in Italian cooking, is: don't cut it! When cut, basil releases too much of its oils, which can make it bitter and drown its flavour. Instead, tear it gently to preserve its subtle, fragrant notes. I add whole leaves towards the end of cooking so the aroma remains strong and it doesn't wilt from being cooked too long. If you are using basil as a garnish, simply tear or leave it whole and add leaves just before serving to maintain its vibrant taste.

KEEPING IT SEASONAL

Eating with the seasons isn't just about using the freshest produce; it's about honouring what the earth gives us naturally throughout the year – there's really no better way to nourish your body. Nonna Igea taught me that you only need what's in season – and a bit of creativity – to make a delicious, wholesome meal.

That's how Nonna works – if something's in season and abundant, you use it, no questions asked. She doesn't even consider buying out-of-season ingredients from the supermarket. For her, food should follow the rhythm of nature, and that means enjoying what's fresh and available at the time. She also knows what's in season and when: ask her about any vegetable and she'll be able to tell you without hesitation. I'll never forget the year we had an abundance of artichokes. She cooked them in so many ways, I thought they might become a permanent fixture on our plates!

MEASUREMENTS

When it comes to Nonna Igea's recipes, don't get too hung up on exact measurements. While it's good to stick close, take inspiration from how she 'just knows' and trusts her instincts. Let your tastebuds and the texture in your hands guide you – unless you're baking and it needs to be a little more precise. And remember, cooking is all about feeling the love, not stressing over the details.

Throughout the book, you'll find many ingredients measured 'qb'. This is an Italian measurement – *quanto basta* – that means 'just enough' or 'to taste' and is commonly used in Italian recipes. Trust your own instincts and measure those ingredients to your preferred taste!

When making pasta, Nonna has been using the ratio of 1 egg per 100g flour forever, but has never actually measured anything, so one day we tested her. Each time she picked up flour to add it to the board where she was preparing the pasta, we measured it and each handful of flour she added was 98–105g – exactly what it should be. It's no wonder nonnas say they don't need measurements! A little more, a little less, they just feel it in their hands. Be guided by this rather than perfection, and each time the final result will continue to get better.

When we're making pasta back in Australia, we often imagine that we are in Nonna's kitchen in Italy, hoping it will influence the end result. Ours isn't always perfect, but that's OK, because we hear her voice saying, '*piano, piano*', which means 'slowly, slowly', as she reminds us that, with time, we will get there. Even if our pasta is not exactly like hers, it will be our version of what she has passed down, and in some ways that is an even better result.

LESS IS MORE

If it's not on the ingredients list, don't add it. Far too many Italian recipes have been ruined by people trying to 'improve' them. In nine times out of ten, these additions throw off the balance of flavours, leaving me wondering what the point was. The concepts of *cucina povera* (poor kitchen) and slow cooking are at the heart of Italian cuisine. Use what you have on hand – and if you grow it yourself, even better! Don't cut corners. Get it right the first time and double the batch so that you have leftovers to freeze for another day, or so that – just like Nonna – you'll always be prepared for unexpected visitors.

MORE CHEESE?

For me? Always. It's a personal preference, of course, but honestly, with all the cheese we eat, we should probably just move to a dairy farm to fuel our cheese addiction. (Like I always say: 'No pecorino, no party'.)

TAKE IT SLOW AND MAKE IT WITH LOVE

If there's one thing to take away, it's this: at the heart of everything we do is pure enjoyment. It's a feeling that's hard to describe in today's fast-paced world, where we're always rushing and pushing ourselves. If you don't have passion and love when making a dish, it's better you don't make it at all. Ingredients can be swapped, but passion is non-negotiable. And take your time when eating, too. We like to enjoy our meals slowly, to savour the flavours. Of course, when dining out, that's the goal – unless our two boys are at the table, then it's more about who can make the most noise, spill the most food, and not sit still for longer than five minutes ... but you know what I mean!

ANTIPASTI

ANTIPASTI

For us, antipasti are more than just a prelude to the main meal, they're a feast of profound flavours, aromas and connections, and our favourite course, especially when dining out. Vincenzo and I often order antipasti in excess, filling our table with an array of small plates that provide an overwhelming sense of joy with each mouthful. Our mantra is: why settle for one dish when you can encourage your taste buds to dance with a delightful medley of bites instead?

Eating antipasti is like a ritual, a moment of bliss. It conjures memories of devouring cheese and salumi, mini pizze fritte (fried pizzas), stuffed vegetables, fried seafood and endless items oozing with melted cheese. It's our goal to keep these mouth-watering moments alive by sharing authentic recipes we entrust to you and your families, to recreate.

Our love for antipasti reached a peak at our wedding in Italy, where 70 starters were sprawled over seemingly infinite tables. Our guests were eager to devour them as the entire meal – except the native Italians, of course, who were used to seeing a spread like that and knew it was just the beginning of the event's culinary component!

Memories of our nonni preparing for the arrival of guests by frying up morsels of dough or squeezing homegrown tomatoes onto fresh bread go hand in hand with our love for antipasti. What is so remarkable is that all of it has always been made effortlessly. For their generation, this sort of preparation and any cooking involved was an honour, because someone had come to visit. They had chosen to spend their precious time together. Nonni went to every effort to show gratitude through a mutual love of food.

We want to instil these values in our children – for them to be able to comprehend the love and bonds that visiting a loved one can bring, and heighten emotions by sharing incredible food. For our nonni, this was always top of mind because, quite simply, it's how it's meant to be.

INSALATA CAPRESE — TOMATO, BASIL AND MOZZARELLA SALAD

Vincenzo likes to refer to the Caprese as the Italian flag on a plate. For me it signifies summer in Italy and the essence of the Mediterranean diet. A simple antipasto salad that can be plated up a few different ways, but the important step (which reigns true in all recipes) is in sourcing the freshest ingredients. With just a handful of elements, this dish demonstrates the beauty of letting fresh, seasonal produce and high-quality staples really show off. If you have never tasted fresh, soft mozzarella, you need to ... now! Then, grab yourself an extra one and slice it up to serve next to slices of heirloom tomato and fresh basil. It is a recipe for one, two or many. This humble dish is a celebration of Italy in so many ways – most especially our love affair with tomatoes!

SERVES 6–8
4 medium heirloom tomatoes, cut into 1cm (½ inch) slices
8–10 small tomatoes such as cherry or grape, halved
2 buffalo mozzarella balls, torn into small chunks
small bunch of fresh basil, qb
salt and pepper
extra virgin olive oil (EVOO), qb

METHOD

1 To assemble, place the tomatoes on the serving plate, then scatter basil leaves over the top.

2 Scatter the mozzarella over and between the tomatoes.

3 Sprinkle with salt and pepper, then drizzle a generous amount of EVOO on top and serve immediately.

VINCENZO'S TIPS
- Do not use hard cheeses you might find in the supermarket that have 'mozzarella' written on them. They are NOT mozzarella, and we can't be friends if you choose these over the real deal! Fresh mozzarella balls are immersed in water and can be found either at the deli or fridge section of your local grocer.
- When using, let the mozzarella drain for a few minutes after slicing. This prevents the salad from becoming watery.
- As much as possible, slice the tomatoes and tear the mozzarella to even thicknesses to guarantee each bite is balanced in flavour and texture.
- The drizzle of EVOO over the top makes all the difference, so don't forget this step. Do it just before serving, so the plate glistens as you bring it to the table and it's still sitting on top.

MELANZANE RIPIENE STUFFED EGGPLANTS

Passed down from my Nonno Spataro, this eggplant recipe is a family treasure. The soft flesh is scooped out and mixed with savoury breadcrumbs and herbs to form small, delicious patties, which are then nestled back into their own skins and shallow-fried. It's a recipe I adore, and not a birthday goes by that I don't put in a special request for a big tray just for me! Making these in our kitchen conjures up so many memories for us, especially of the home-grown eggplants we got to share with Nonno before he passed. While mine may never taste quite as good as Mamma Maria's, I'll keep practising. Hopefully, one day my kids will love them just as much as I do – at the moment, it's a work in progress!

MAKES 12

3 medium eggplants (aubergines)
½ tbsp salt
1½ cups (120g/4.5 oz) fresh breadcrumbs
½ cup (45g/1.6 oz) finely grated Pecorino Romano, plus extra for sprinkling
small bunch flat-leaf (Italian) parsley, leaves finely chopped
3 garlic cloves, finely chopped
1 egg
olive oil, for shallow-frying

METHOD

1 Quarter the eggplants by cutting in half lengthwise, then widthwise. Score the inside edges of each quarter using a sharp knife. This will help the skin stay on while cooking and allow you to easily remove it once ready.

2 Fill a large saucepan with water and immerse the eggplant, then place over medium heat. Add the salt. Bring to the boil and cook until fork-tender, before removing and straining. Leave to cool, then carefully carve out the pulp, reserving the skins. Cut the pulp into small pieces. Combine with the breadcrumbs, Pecorino, parsley, garlic and egg in a bowl.

3 Pat down each eggplant skin to remove any moisture. Using your hands, pick up a portion of the mixture and shape into a small patty. Place it on top of the skin, pressing down firmly and keeping each roughly the same size. Repeat until each skin is filled, then place in the fridge, covered, for 30 minutes to set.

4 Heat a frying pan over medium–low heat. Add a generous drizzle of oil. When it is warm, shallow-fry the patties, stuffing-side down, in batches if necessary. Leave to cook for 1–2 minutes, then turn over and cook through. Be careful not to burn the skin as this side won't take as long to cook once you turn it.

5 Remove the skin from each patty and transfer to a plate lined with paper towel. Fry the side of the patty that is not cooked, then transfer to the plate too. Once the excess oil has been absorbed, arrange each patty back on a skin. Sprinkle with extra Pecorino before serving.

MAMMA MARIA'S TIPS

- Adjust the size you cut the eggplants into based on what's available. After boiling, you can trim the skin if needed to keep the portions consistent with the patties.
- When separating the skin from the pulp, don't scrape too close to the skin as it will dry up when cooked. There should be a thin layer of flesh so it remains tender.
- While Nonno Spataro always placed the patties in the eggplant skin, you don't have to – but this is a reminder that in Italian cooking, especially these cucina povera–style recipes, nothing goes to waste.
- Always fry one patty through first, then cut it in half and taste it to make sure it is to your desired texture. The patty consistency is dependent on the amount of breadcrumbs and cheese added, and if you make the patties larger, they will take a little longer to cook through. If you find they are too hard or dry once cooked, use less of the breadcrumbs next time. If they are too soft, and crumble easily, add less cheese.

BRUSCHETTA DI POMODORO TOMATO BRUSCHETTA

Bruschetta isn't just a slice of bread with tomatoes; it's a taste of Italy's history, rooted in simplicity and tradition. Picture farmers in the Italian countryside, taking yesterday's bread and transforming it with fresh-pressed olive oil and sun-warmed tomatoes, the flavours mingling as they soak into every golden, crunchy bite.

In my family, we made bruschetta with *biscotto di grano* (or *viscotto*, as we called it), a hard Calabrian bread softened with water, drenched in olive oil and topped with tomatoes and basil picked that day from Nonno's garden. Each bite was better than the last – rich, fragrant and bursting with sweet tomato juice. Vincenzo's version is the classic one, but still just as sensational.

SERVES 4 AS A SIDE
2–3 ripe tomatoes
extra virgin olive oil (EVOO), qb
salt and pepper
2 garlic cloves, peeled, 1 crushed, 1 whole, for rubbing
small handful of basil leaves
4 slices sourdough or pane di casa, 1–1.5cm (½ inch) thick

METHOD

1 Roughly chop the tomatoes directly into a bowl to catch every ounce of juice – messy but worth it. Add a generous amount of EVOO, salt, pepper and the crushed garlic. Reserve 2 basil leaves for garnishing, then add the rest, breaking the leaves into smaller pieces with your hands or leaving them whole. Just please don't cut them (or argue about why with an Italian!). Mix together using your hands or a spoon and leave for 10–20 minutes to rest at room temperature.

2 Tomato bruschetta should be served on golden, crispy bread. Prepare by adding slices of bread to a hot barbecue grill and cook on both sides to the desired texture – you can easily make the bread softer or harder this way and likely not overdo it. Lightly charred is best. Once the bread is ready and still hot, rub the extra garlic clove on one side and allow it to slightly melt.

3 Place the bread on a large chopping board, garlic side facing up. Using a tablespoon, scoop up juice from the bowl of tomato mixture and pour it over each slice of bread, before adding the tomato mixture, more juice and the reserved basil leaves, torn roughly. You can also drizzle some more EVOO on top because honestly, is there really ever enough?

VINCENZO'S TIPS

- If you can't find fresh tomatoes, it's probably best not to make it this way and experiment with another topping instead. Make this your own by choosing seafood, pickled vegetables or even cheeses as a substitute.
- For a fresh, herby alternative, spread a thin layer of pesto on the bread before adding toppings. Pesto enhances the bruschetta with notes of rich basil and garlic. You only need to add melted mozzarella on top.
- If you're Calabrese, finely diced red onion in place of the garlic is absolutely acceptable.
- There are a few rules to follow, but bruschetta comes from the word *bruscare*, meaning to 'roast over coals'. So the message here? Toast your bread well.
- Most bread varieties will work, but my favourites are sourdough and pane di casa. Unlike the tomatoes, the bread doesn't need to be fresh. In fact, if it's a little stale it's probably perfect.

FRITTELLE DI ZUCCHINE ZUCCHINI FRITTERS

These bite-sized pieces of fried zucchini goodness are made in several regions and are also known as *pitteri* in my family. This scrumptious recipe is from my mamma, Maria, whose parents hail from Calabria. They immigrated to Australia many years ago, bringing with them a legacy of southern Italian recipes that they faithfully prepared for their table every single day.

Mamma is by far the queen of zucchini fritters in our family and her recipe went viral on social media when Vincenzo first posted it years ago, amassing millions of views ... and honestly, it's no wonder. Everyone in our family loves them! One of my fondest memories is from when we visited Pescara as a family in 2013 and Mamma made them to accompany one of our meals. No one could stop at just one (though Nonna Igea made her own version shortly after to share her recipe too).

SERVES 8 AS A SIDE

5 medium zucchini (courgettes), finely grated
table (fine) salt
5 eggs
pepper
3 heaped tbsp self-raising (rising) flour
2 heaped tbsp plain (all-purpose) flour
5 tbsp finely grated Pecorino Romano, plus extra for sprinkling
olive oil, for frying

METHOD

1 Place the zucchini in a bowl, sprinkle with salt and leave for at least 10 minutes to rest. Then scoop out a handful of the zucchini at a time and squeeze it over the sink by pressing both hands around it until you get all the water out before transferring to a clean bowl.

2 Crack the eggs into a separate bowl and whisk well. Add salt and pepper and mix again. Mix in both flours and the Pecorino, then transfer the mixture to the bowl of zucchini and mix together.

3 Drizzle some oil into a frying pan (just enough to shallow-fry the fritters) and heat over medium heat. Once ready, turn the temperature down slightly so the oil doesn't burn. In batches, scoop out heaped tablespoons of the zucchini mixture and gently drop them into the oil, leaving space in between. Cook each side for just over a minute, or until golden brown. The cooking time may vary depending on the amount of mixture you add in and how hot the oil is. Taste one while cooking to make sure the centre is cooked through and not runny; otherwise lower the heat and fry a little longer. Remove each fritter once cooked and transfer to a plate lined with paper towel to absorb any excess oil.

4 To serve, arrange on a large platter and sprinkle extra Pecorino on top. Don't miss this step – the saltiness of the cheese balances out the flavour.

MAMMA MARIA'S TIPS

- When preparing the zucchini, squeeze out as much of the water as possible. You'll likely need to do this more than once for each handful to release all of the liquid. Use a muslin (cheesecloth) if you have one.
- For even cooking, try to make all the fritters roughly the same size. But remember, the beauty of homemade cooking is that no two will ever be exactly the same, so don't try too hard.
- While I use olive oil for cooking these, EVOO also works.
- Cook the fritters in batches to ensure they fry evenly and the oil temperature doesn't drop too much.

MOZZARELLA IN CARROZZA — FRIED MOZZARELLA SANDWICHES

The O.G. grilled cheese toastie. Mozzarella in carrozza is a classic southern Italian street food born in the fried-snack capital, Naples. A masterpiece of crispy, golden-fried bread giving way to a warm, unmistakable river of melted, stringy mozzarella, it is so much more than a toasted sandwich. Vincenzo is incredibly talented at making this, which I attribute to his strong passion (obsession?) for cheese. Indulge yourself with this savoury, irresistible treat – just be sure to devour it hot, and if she's nearby, share with Nonna!

SERVES 6 AS A SIDE (3 SANDWICHES)

3 eggs
salt and pepper
100g (3.5 oz) plain (all-purpose) flour, for coating
6 slices pane di casa or sourdough bread
1 fresh fior di latte or buffalo mozzarella ball, cut into 1cm (1/2 inch) thick slices
sunflower oil, for deep-frying

METHOD

1 Crack the eggs into a bowl, season with a pinch of salt and a generous amount of pepper before beating with a whisk.

2 Place the flour in a wide bowl or on a flat plate and place each slice of bread on top, pressing down so it is covered, then repeat on the other side before shaking off any excess. Place on a plate lined with baking (parchment) paper.

3 Dip the floured bread into the egg mixture on one side only, then rest it on the paper, wet side facing up. Dip both sides of the mozzarella slices into the egg, then place three on each bread slice, using half circles of mozzarella if you need to, so the whole piece of bread is covered. Put the second bread slice on top, wet side facing down, then press down firmly with your hands, including on the ends. Repeat for all sandwiches.

4 Dip an entire sandwich into the egg mixture, allowing the excess egg to drip back into the bowl. Make sure you cover all sides (even the crust) to seal in the cheese. This is a really important step, so cover every inch! Place on a plate lined with baking (parchment) paper. Repeat with the remaining sandwiches, then place the plate in the fridge for 20–30 minutes to set.

5 Just before the resting time is up, heat a generous amount of oil in a frying pan until it reaches 180°C (360°F) or small bubbles appear around the handle of a wooden spoon.

6 Add one sandwich to the pan and cook until golden and crispy on one side. Use a spoon to gently keep covering the top of the sandwich with oil, then turn over and repeat until golden and crispy. Repeat with the remaining sandwiches. Place on a plate lined with paper towel. Use paper towel to blot excess oil off the top, then enjoy every crunchy bite – preferably while it's still hot, but not sizzling.

VINCENZO'S TIPS

- Don't slice the mozzarella any thicker than 1cm (1/2 inch) or it won't melt.
- Use one egg per sandwich as a measurement to increase/decrease the quantity you make.
- You can remove the crust, but I prefer it rustic and crunchy, so ours stays on.
- Once you have closed the sandwich, press down enough to seal in the cheese, so it doesn't ooze out while cooking.
- If you find the bread is burning before the cheese melts, you can turn down the heat to medium–low.

POMODORI RIPIENI DI NONNO SPATARO — STUFFED TOMATOES

Growing up just streets away from my nonni, we were often together for meals. As they grew older, my Nonno Spataro took on more of the cooking, often with the unmistakable quality produce from his own garden. The vegetable patch he curated was more than just a hobby, it was his pride and joy. Nonno's specialties were eggplant, broccoli and his beloved tomatoes. In summer, he would pick the smaller ones and leave them to over-ripen to perfection. That's when he would make this variation of the signature dish known as *pomodori chini alla Calabrese* in Calabrese dialect. Typical of Calabria, these patties stuffed with cheese, breadcrumbs and tomato pulp are then moulded to size and sit on a bed of tomato skin. Originally a dish made at the end of summer with kitchen leftovers, today it's a true delicacy – a taste of Nonno's love and the seasons all wrapped in one bite. Nonno would make these so effortlessly, then hardly eat any, just wanting the family to enjoy them.

SERVES 4–8 AS A SIDE
- 8 small ripe tomatoes, halved lengthways
- salt and pepper
- 1 cup (80g/2.8 oz) fresh breadcrumbs, plus extra if needed
- ½ cup (45g/1.6 oz) finely grated Pecorino Romano, plus extra for sprinkling
- 6–8 basil leaves, roughly torn into small pieces
- 3 garlic cloves, finely chopped
- 1 egg
- olive oil, for shallow-frying

METHOD

1 Score the pulp out of the tomato halves and place the pulp into a sieve set over a bowl. If there is still any juice inside, empty it into the bowl. (Haven't you learnt by now? Don't waste a thing!) Then sprinkle a little salt into each tomato skin and set aside.

2 Squash the pulp through the sieve with your hands, or the back of a spoon, so the juice drains into the bowl and the seeds are left behind. (Dry the seeds on a paper towel and use them for next season's crop.) Add the breadcrumbs, Pecorino, basil, garlic and egg to the bowl, season with salt and pepper, then mix. If the filling is too soft and wet, add more breadcrumbs and continue to mix with your hands so it combines well.

3 Still using your hands, scoop up an eighth of the mixture and make a patty to fit into one of the tomato skin bases you cut earlier. Press the patty, so it is compact and not crumbling or falling apart, before placing it into the tomato skin. Repeat for the remaining tomatoes. Place the stuffed tomatoes on a flat plate and refrigerate for at least 30 minutes.

4 Heat a frying pan over medium heat and add a generous drizzle of oil. Once the pan is warm, shallow-fry the stuffed tomatoes, skin facing up, in batches until golden and a little crispy. Turn over and fry the other side until the tomato skin is soft and slightly crinkled. Transfer to a plate lined with paper towel to drain. Arrange the tomatoes on a serving plate and sprinkle with Pecorino.

NONNO SPATARO'S TIPS
- Choose tomatoes that are well ripened but not too squishy, as you want the sweetness of the juice when using the pulp.
- Size-wise, the tomatoes should not be too big, as these are delicious served as bite-sized portions.
- Cook each patty on one side in the pan, allowing the heat to cook through the tomato skin on the other side. The top will be crispy, while the bottom stays slightly softer. Taste the first one to check the texture before cooking the rest.

FIORI DI ZUCCA RIPIENI — STUFFED ZUCCHINI FLOWERS

Preparing zucchini flowers requires a dash of patience, but they aren't difficult to make. These are a classic Italian delicacy with fillings that vary by region. Vincenzo's favourite is a mix of ricotta and gorgonzola, with a little lemon zest and a pinch of nutmeg (a combination that makes him burst into song, literally!). While zucchini flowers can be a challenge to find, you'll have the best luck at farmers' markets during spring. And just like Nonna would remind you, never waste food. Use any leftover filling for fresh ravioli (see recipe, page 87–8) or as a bruschetta topping (see recipe, page 26).

SERVES 4–8 AS A SIDE

- 8 zucchini (courgette) flowers
- sparkling water, chilled, for soaking and mixing
- 250g (8.8 oz) fresh ricotta
- 3 tbsp gorgonzola
- zest of 1 lemon
- sprinkle of nutmeg
- 1 egg
- 1 cup (150g/5.3 oz) plain (all-purpose) flour, plus extra for coating
- sunflower oil, for shallow-frying
- lemon wedges, to serve
- rock salt

METHOD

1 To prepare zucchini flowers, remove the pistil or stamen from the middle using your index finger and thumb, then discard. Place the flowers in a bowl of sparkling water to soak.

2 Using a fork, combine the ricotta, gorgonzola and lemon zest in a large bowl, pressing down on the ricotta. Mix in the nutmeg, then a splash of sparkling water. Continue gradually adding more sparkling water until creamy, but not runny.

3 Spoon the mixture into a sealable plastic bag, then close and push the mixture to one corner, before cutting a small hole. (Alternatively, use a piping bag or simply fill using a spoon.)

4 Beat the egg in a bowl, then add the flour and some sparkling water. The consistency should be creamy and thick. Add extra flour if it's watery, or sparkling water if it's too thick.

5 Remove a flower from the water. Shake gently to remove excess water or pat dry with paper towel. Pipe about a tablespoon of ricotta mixture into the flower. Cross each petal over the top of your filling so it is sealed, and with the leftover length, twist them together and press lightly so it remains closed. Dip into a bowl of extra flour and transfer to a large plate or tray to rest. Repeat with the remaining flowers.

6 Add oil to a frying pan so it's 1–2cm (½–¾ in) deep and heat until it reaches 180°C (360°F) or small bubbles appear around the handle of a wooden spoon. Position the batter near the pan. Dip each flower into the batter, let any excess drip off, then lower it carefully into the oil. Fry two to three flowers at a time (to avoid overcrowding), turning frequently with a slotted spoon, until golden and crisp. Transfer to a plate or tray lined with paper towel to drain.

7 Arrange on a platter with lemon wedges and a sprinkle of rock salt. Serve immediately.

VINCENZO'S TIPS

- Soaking the flowers is a key step, so the petals soften enough to fold over one another.
- Add as much lemon zest to the filling as you like. It pairs well with this cheese filling, and I like to say, 'No lemon, no party!'
- When transferring the flowers to the pan, some excess batter might drop in. Try to remove it so it doesn't burn and change the taste of the oil.
- If the flowers aren't well sealed, filling might escape into the pan, making a mess or letting oil seep into the filling. If this happens, let it cook, then seal the others more tightly.

CAPONATA SICILIANA — SICILIAN EGGPLANT SALAD

This Sicilian tradition is a delicious vegan relish that's authentically Italian and absolutely unforgettable. A vibrant mix of golden fried eggplants, slow-cooked passata, olives, capers and pine nuts creates a flavour eruption, much like Mount Etna itself! We always make extra when this is on the menu because it's hard to resist and we devour it on crostini before it even hits the table. After shooting this dish for the book, we all grabbed spoons and fresh bread. By the time we were done, you couldn't even tell the pan had been used. We mopped up every last drop of sauce.

SERVES 4 AS A SIDE

- 500g (17.6 oz) eggplant (aubergine), trimmed and cut into small cubes
- salt
- sunflower oil, for frying
- 120ml (4 fl oz) extra virgin olive oil (EVOO)
- ½ red onion, finely chopped
- 2 celery stalks, finely sliced
- 100ml (3.4 fl oz) tomato passata or use homemade (see recipe, page 74)
- 2 tbsp salted capers or caperberries, rinsed
- 12 pitted green olives, halved
- 200g (7 oz) cherry tomatoes, halved
- small bunch of basil, leaves torn
- 30g (1 oz) pine nuts, toasted

AGRODOLCE

- 2 tbsp sugar
- 5 tbsp (100ml/3.5 fl oz) red wine vinegar

METHOD

1 Place the eggplant in a strainer set over a large bowl to catch the water. Sprinkle with salt, mix well, and repeat with another sprinkle. Let it sit for at least an hour to strain, or overnight for best results.

2 Discard the strained water, and pat dry the eggplant with paper towel. Heat a generous drizzle of sunflower oil in a large frying pan over medium heat. Fry the eggplant for about 5 minutes, or until golden and slightly crispy. Transfer to a plate or tray lined with paper towel to drain.

3 Heat the EVOO in a large saucepan or Dutch oven over medium heat. Add the onion and celery and simmer, stirring occasionally, for 5–7 minutes or until tender and glossy. Using a wooden spoon, stir in the passata and a pinch of salt. Add the capers, olives and cherry tomatoes. Reduce heat to medium–low and cook, stirring occasionally, for 5 minutes, or until the tomato begins to blister. Add the eggplant and cook over low heat for 2 minutes. Add the basil and cook for another 2 minutes.

4 Meanwhile, for the agrodolce, combine the sugar and vinegar in a small saucepan over medium–low heat, stirring, until the sugar dissolves, then remove from the heat. Add this to the tomato mixture, stir with the wooden spoon until well combined, then mix in the pine nuts. Turn off the heat and set aside to cool.

5 Once rested, chill in the fridge (it's best served cold). Enjoy as a bruschetta topping (see recipe, page 26), as a side to lamb or on its own. Scoop it up *alla scarpetta*, with bread instead of a spoon!

VINCENZO'S TIPS

- In regions like Palermo, fresh tomatoes are used instead of passata. Peel, deseed and dice 6–8 tomatoes, then add to a saucepan with EVOO and thinly sliced onion. Simmer until the tomato is half-cooked, then use as the base for your caponata.
- To toast the pine nuts, prepare a baking tray with baking (parchment) paper and spread out evenly. Bake in a 150°C (300°F) oven until golden, being careful not to overcook – keep an eye on them as they can easily burn. Remove from the oven once they start to turn golden and a beautiful aroma fills the kitchen.

CALAMARI FRITTI FRIED CALAMARI

This may surprise some, but I'm not sure I would call fried calamari an uber-traditional Italian dish. It is, however, a classic in the sense that it's always on the menu of Italian restaurants (globally). Outside Italy, fried calamari is served as an antipasto dish, but in Italy it is typically served alongside other seafood as a *secondo piatto* near the end of your meal. This dish is known as *fritto misto di mare* (mixed fried seafood). Vincenzo's recipe creates golden, crispy calamari rings, using semolina and a lemon marinade that produces the perfect amount of crunch and zest. Just try and enjoy this dish at a restaurant after you've tasted his version. It's also one of our eldest son Sebastian's favourite dishes, so is on repeat in our kitchen!

SERVES 4 AS A SIDE
3–4 freshly cleaned calamari, including tentacles
1–2 lemons
3 tbsp finely chopped flat-leaf (Italian) parsley leaves, plus extra to serve
2½ cups fine semolina
salt and pepper
sunflower oil, for deep-frying

METHOD

1 Lay the calamari flat on a chopping board and, using a sharp knife or kitchen scissors, cut into rings and transfer to a bowl. Cut the tentacles in halves or thirds and add to the bowl.

2 Squeeze the juice of 1 lemon half over the calamari. Add 1 tsp parsley and mix so the calamari begins to marinate. This adds to their zesty flavour and softens them slightly too.

3 In another bowl, combine the semolina and remaining parsley. A little extra parsley is fine so don't worry about measuring. Season with salt and pepper.

4 Once the calamari have marinated for a few minutes, drain slightly. Add to flour mixture.

5 Pour a generous amount of oil into a frying pan and heat until it reaches 180°C (360°F) or small bubbles appear around the handle of a wooden spoon.

6 While waiting for the oil to heat up, mix the calamari until each piece is completely covered in the semolina mixture and doesn't feel wet. Again, leave for a couple of minutes to set. Place the calamari in a sieve and shake gently to remove any excess semolina mixture.

7 Once the oil is ready, drop in the calamari, a few at a time depending on the size of the pan. Fry for 60–90 seconds, or until the outer layer becomes crispy. Once the calamari are crisp and golden, strain using a skimmer or sieve and transfer to a plate lined with paper towel to soak up any excess oil.

8 Serve garnished with extra parsley and the remaining lemon cut into wedges.

VINCENZO'S TIPS
- When cutting the calamari, make sure the strips or rings are not too thick as they can end up being chewy. Kitchen scissors are an easy way to cut more consistently.
- Calamari should be fried briefly. Overcooking will make them rubbery, so do a taste test once you have fried up the first batch to check texture.
- Don't overcrowd the pan when frying, as this will lower the oil temperature and cause the calamari to become soggy and potentially not cook through. Fry in small batches to maintain a consistent high heat.
- Let guests squeeze their own lemon to keep the calamari fresh and crisp.
- To make fritto misto you can also add sardines and anchovies, or if you want larger portions, barramundi and whiting work well too.

INSALATA DI BRESAOLA BRESAOLA SALAD

When we talk about Italian cooking, the trick to creating a fantastic dish is really about using premium ingredients. This bresaola salad is no exception. Very little preparation (that is, none!) is required to create this Tuscan-inspired recipe. It will surprise you in the best possible way, with every sweet and salty mouthful.

Bresaola is one of the only salumi made from beef and it is the leanest (and most aesthetically pleasing) cut. It is a little pricier compared to other cuts, but don't be deterred, as it is sliced very thinly and you don't need a large amount.

When Vincenzo introduced me to this salad, I remember eating most of the serving myself – it was so addictive I couldn't get enough. The paper-thin slices of umami-packed bresaola mixed with lemon, balsamic and olive oil make for a fast salad full of flavour.

This is a refreshing antipasto dish, but can also accompany a main course. If you prep ahead, the exposure to air can change the appearance and colour of the bresaola, so have the dressing and ingredients ready and plate it up just moments before serving.

SERVES 4

- 50–80ml (1.7–2.7 fl oz) extra virgin olive oil (EVOO)
- 80–100ml (1.7–2.7 fl oz) balsamic vinegar
- 1 lemon, halved
- 2 lightly packed cups (50g/1.7 oz) rocket (arugula), washed and patted dry
- sea salt and pepper
- 100–150g (3.5–5.3 oz) bresaola, thinly sliced
- 50–100g (1.7–3.5 oz) Parmigiano Reggiano
- balsamic glaze (optional)

METHOD

1 To prepare the dressing, pour the EVOO into a jar or glass along with the balsamic vinegar. Squeeze the juice of 1 lemon half into the jar (making sure no seeds fall in), put on the lid and shake well.

2 Place the rocket into a bowl, sprinkle with a pinch of salt and pepper, then add the dressing, mixing it in with your hands.

3 Start by arranging the bresaola in a circle around the rim of a flat plate (or chopping board), overlapping slightly. Continue layering until the plate or board is covered. Using your hands, pile the rocket in the centre, allowing the bresaola to peek out around the edges.

4 Shave the cheese over the salad, letting both thin and thick pieces and crumbs fall on top. Squeeze the remaining lemon half over, watching out for seeds. For extra richness and colour, drizzle a touch of balsamic glaze.

VINCENZO'S TIPS

- Use organic lemons, if possible. The flavour of the juice is much sweeter than you think, and will help you create a salad even closer to what is served in Italy.
- A good substitute for rocket is baby spinach, but it doesn't have the same peppery taste, so try both and pick your preference. For me, there's not much like this salad combination with rocket.
- Look for high-quality bresaola that is thinly sliced. It should have a rich red colour and be free of any excessive fatty edges.
- To keep the rocket crisp, dress the salad just before serving. This prevents the leaves from wilting under the dressing.

PANZEROTTI PUGLIESI PIZZA POCKETS FROM PUGLIA

Panzerotti are half-moon-shaped fried pizza-dough pockets, filled to the brim with flavour. Originally from Puglia, they are an irrefutable, irresistible street food you must try. Can't get to Puglia? Make this recipe! This traditional version is courtesy of Vincenzo's foodie friend Ottavio. He was taught by Nonna Bellina growing up in Puglia, so don't even consider questioning its authenticity! She filled her version with sweet, crushed San Marzano tomatoes, gooey mozzarella and capers, and now, so do we.

SERVES 6

700g (24.7 oz) plain (all-purpose) flour, plus extra for dusting
300g (10.6 oz) semolina
3 tbsp (40g/1.4 oz) table (fine) salt
2 tbsp (20g/0.7 oz) white sugar
700ml (23.7 fl oz) full cream milk, plus extra if needed
2 tbsp (20g/0.7 oz) fresh yeast
1 tbsp (20ml/0.7 fl oz) extra virgin olive oil (EVOO)
1 fresh fior di latte mozzarella ball, diced
1 × 400g (14 oz) canned crushed Italian tomatoes
24–30 capers
Parmigiano Reggiano, grated
sunflower oil, for shallow-frying

SPECIAL EQUIPMENT
dough cutter or scraper

METHOD

1 Mix the flour, semolina, salt and sugar on a clean wooden bench. Make a deep well in the middle and pour in the milk. Add the yeast and dissolve with your hands. Mix by working your way around the well and pushing the flour into it. Do this until milk absorbs and mixture starts to feel gooey. Keep combining until a dough forms. Add a splash of extra milk if too dry or extra flour if too sticky. Knead for 10 minutes, pushing it back and forward on your surface. When kneading forward, fold the top part over, then push again. Repeat until you can poke a finger into the ball and it springs back. (Vincenzo says to be passionate when kneading, as though you're making love to the dough. It needs to feel your emotions and will always turn out just right.)

2 Drizzle up to 1 tbsp EVOO over the ball of dough and roll it around so it's completely covered, then knead it again for a few minutes until the oil soaks in. Using a dough cutter or scraper, cut the dough into six portions weighing 120–140g (4.2–5 oz), which is the perfect size for one panzerotto. Roll each one into a ball. After creating the balls leave them on your bench covered with a sheet of baking (parchment) paper and a tea towel for up to 3 hours or until they double in size.

3 Sprinkle extra flour over the bench and place one ball on top. Using a rolling pin, start to flatten the ball by rolling back and forth until round, flat and 4mm (1/8 in) thick. Place a few pieces of mozzarella in the centre of the dough round. Add 3 tbsp tomato, 4–5 capers and a sprinkle of Parmigiano. Fold one side of dough down on top of the other, joining the edges, and press firmly, making sure it's sealed airtight. Repeat until you have used all your dough balls.

4 Pour a generous amount of oil into a frying pan and heat until it reaches 180°C (360°F) or small bubbles appear around the handle of a wooden spoon. Once the oil is hot, lower one panzerotto gently into the oil. Let it cook for 1½ minutes, using a spoon to gently keep covering the top with oil and moving it around. Flip and cook on the other side for 1 minute, then back to the first side for another minute until each side is lightly golden. Remove and drain on a plate lined with paper towel. Repeat with the remaining panzerotti. Serve while hot, but be careful not to burn yourself!

OTTAVIO'S TIPS
- To seal each panzerotto even more securely, use an egg wash (beaten egg with milk). Lather on the dough edges with a pastry brush, then close tightly.
- Lower the panzerotti into the pan middle-first, then gently lower each side. This helps prevent it breaking.
- Fill with whatever you like. Experiment with different fillings, like ham and cheese, spinach and ricotta, or for a sweet twist, try chocolate spread or fruit jam.

PALLOTTE CACIO E OVE PECORINO CHEESE BALLS

This dish was born years ago in Vincenzo's home region of Abruzzo and was created by mixing a few readily available ingredients. Not a lot to it, just stale bread, cheese and eggs. Yet while the combination may sound unassuming, there is a reason they are served at every authentic trattoria in the region. There is rife competition about who has the superior recipe, not to mention within families too – ours included! But I have to say, Vincenzo's recipe is the ultimate, and these are 100 per cent Nonna Igea approved. When you look at them and slide your fork in, you will be forgiven for thinking they are made with meat! The texture comes from a combination of stale bread and Abruzzo's most famous, and Vincenzo's favourite, cheese: PECORINO.

MAKES 12–14 BALLS (2 PER PERSON MINIMUM)
400g (14 oz) Pecorino Romano, finely grated
2 heaped tbsp breadcrumbs
small bunch of flat-leaf (Italian) parsley, leaves finely chopped
salt and pepper
4 eggs
2–4 slices stale pane di casa bread, crusts off
olive or sunflower oil, for deep-frying

SIMPLE SUGO
¼–⅓ cup (60–80ml/2–2.7 fl oz) extra virgin olive oil (EVOO)
1 garlic clove, crushed
500g (17.6 oz) tomato passata or use homemade (see recipe, page 74)
salt
small handful of basil leaves

METHOD

1 For the sugo, heat a saucepan over medium heat. Add the EVOO and garlic. Once the garlic starts to become translucent, add the passata and a pinch of salt. Leave to simmer gently, stirring occasionally, for 15 minutes, then switch off heat and set aside.

2 Meanwhile, for the cheese balls, add the Pecorino, breadcrumbs, parsley, salt and pepper to a large bowl, and mix well using a tablespoon or your hands. Crack the eggs into the mixture and combine well using a fork.

3 Quickly dip the bread into a bowl filled with water, then squeeze out all the water with your hands. Break into pieces, then add to the egg mixture. Combine using your hands or a fork. Nonna Igea and Vincenzo use their hands; for them there is no other way to know if it is the right texture.

4 Pour a generous amount of oil into a frying pan and heat until it reaches 170°C (340°F) or small bubbles appear around the handle of a wooden spoon.

5 Wet hands slightly, scoop up some mixture using a tablespoon and roll into a ball. Place on a baking (parchment) paper lined-tray. Repeat with the remaining mixture.

6 Once the oil is hot, place a few balls in the pan and cook for 2 minutes, or until golden. Don't overcrowd the pan. Turn each one to ensure it is cooked through.

7 Meanwhile, warm up the sugo over low heat. Add the basil. Once the cheese balls are cooked, they should then be transferred into the warm sugo, completely coated and cooked for at least 5 minutes. This is the most traditional way to serve them. As alternate options, you can also serve them crunchy, with sugo on the side, or simply resting on the sugo. If you choose the third option, serve them right away as they will tend to go soggy on the bottom.

VINCENZO'S TIPS
- The amount of bread you need depends on two things I can't control: the size of the eggs and how much water you squeeze out of the bread. If the consistency feels too wet, add more bread.
- If the oil is too hot, the cheese balls will brown too quickly, leaving the centres uncooked. Avoid overheating the oil and do a taste test with the first few, checking the centres for a soft (not runny) consistency. Halfway through cooking, you may need to turn the heat down so the balls cook consistently.

ZUCCHINE GRIGLIATE GRILLED ZUCCHINI

Grilled zucchini is one of those staples we love to serve as a side or antipasto when hosting a dinner party. While you can dress them simply with a sprinkle of salt and drizzle of oil, this particular recipe is about embracing the versatile vegetable and elevating it. Mixed with crispy whole almonds, fresh mint and drizzled with extra virgin olive oil, Vincenzo's grilled zucchini are the perfect addition to any summer meal and one of the quickest recipes you can make.

Inspired by the incredible flavours of southern Italy, where sun-dried zucchini aplenty can be found at markets, this grilled version turns up the flavour intensity and brings your palette to Sicily. If you want a richer flavour, dice up some dried figs and add them to enhance the flavour profile even more, then top with dollops of creamy stracciatella cheese – *mamma mia*!

SERVES 4 AS A SIDE
3 zucchini (courgettes), cut lengthways into thin slices, about 1cm (½ in)
salt and pepper
bunch of mint
small handful of roasted or raw blanched almonds, roughly chopped

EASY ITALIAN DRESSING
1 garlic clove, crushed
½ cup (125ml/4.2 fl oz) extra virgin olive oil (EVOO)
1 tbsp balsamic vinegar

METHOD

1 Make the dressing by mixing the garlic, EVOO and balsamic in a bowl using a spoon (or add it to a jar and shake well).

2 Warm a skillet or barbecue grill plate over medium-high heat, then add several slices of zucchini, letting them brown slightly on one side.

3 Once they have grill marks, flip the zucchini and cook the other side – don't be afraid to check ahead of time, just try not to handle them too much as they soften quickly. Place on a long chopping board or flat plate. Repeat with the remaining slices.

4 While the next slices are cooking, sprinkle salt and pepper over the first batch, then add a spoonful of the dressing. Add pieces of mint, tearing the leaves with your hands for a rustic look or chopping them finely for a more subtle flavour. Sprinkle almonds over the top. Repeat until all the zucchini is cooked and seasoned, adding the remaining dressing on top.

5 Garnish the zucchini with a few whole or chopped mint leaves. Try to devour each bite by mixing zucchini, crunchy almonds and a touch of dressing.

VINCENZO'S TIPS

- EVOO and balsamic vinegar make all the difference in this dish. Keep in mind that a great balsamic vinegar doesn't need to be expensive, but it should be high quality. If you can find a balsamic vinegar from Modena, invest in it because it is much more intense. Even the slightest drizzle will create maximum impact.
- Don't fall for store-bought 'Italian dressing' – it's a scam! Just make your own with garlic, EVOO and balsamic vinegar. It's fresher, tastier and way better for you.
- If you have any dressing left over, add whole or chopped mint and use it for other salads or grilled vegetables the same day.
- Once grilled, don't leave the zucchini resting too long before you dress and serve them, as they will soften over time. If possible, cut the slices early on but cook at the last minute.

ARANCINI SICILIANI STUFFED RICE BALLS

In Sicily, arancini aren't just a snack, they are a way of life. Each golden, crispy bite reveals a rich, savoury ragu and an unforgettable pocket of oozy, melted cheese. It's a sensory experience that, for us, brings back memories of wandering through Sicily, eating them at every chance we got. Ever since Vincenzo learned the art of arancini, he has been perfecting his Bolognese version.

MAKES 8 ARANCINI
100ml (3.4 fl oz) extra virgin olive oil (EVOO)
¼ onion, chopped
4 cups (1L/33.8 fl oz) vegetable stock
1 tbsp concentrated tomato paste
370g (9.5 oz) butter
500g (17.6 oz) arborio rice
1 cup (90g/3.2 oz) finely grated Pecorino Romano or Parmigiano Reggiano
2 eggs
small bowl of breadcrumbs (fresh if possible!)
sunflower oil, for deep-frying

ARANCINI FILLING
100ml (3.4 fl oz) extra virgin olive oil (EVOO)
1 celery stalk, diced
½ onion, diced
1 carrot, diced
500g (17.6 oz) minced (ground) beef
100g (3.5 oz) fresh or frozen peas
120g (4.2 oz) concentrated tomato paste
handful of basil leaves
1 fresh fior di latte mozzarella ball, diced into small cubes
salt and pepper

METHOD

1 Place a large metal baking tray in the fridge to chill.

2 Heat EVOO in a large saucepan on medium heat. Add the onion, stirring often with a wooden spoon, for 3–5 minutes, or until translucent and starting to brown. Mix in the stock, tomato paste and 120g butter. Bring to the boil. Add the rice, stir quickly, then cover. Cook, stirring frequently and replacing the lid each time, then just before all the liquid is absorbed, reduce heat to medium-low. When the rice is tender and cooked, remove the lid and stir in the remaining butter until melted. Spread the mixture over the chilled tray, using a wooden spoon to spread to the edges (be gentle: the rice can break). Top with cheese. Set aside for 1 hour to cool.

3 For the filling, heat 4–5 tbsp (2–2.5 fl oz) EVOO in a large frying pan over medium heat. Add the celery, onion and carrot. Cook, stirring frequently, for 10 minutes, then add the beef, breaking it up with a wooden spoon, until browned. Stir in the peas, tomato paste, basil and a splash of water until combined. Lower heat and simmer for 20 minutes. Stir in another splash of water, so it doesn't dry out. Season. Transfer to a bowl and chill in the fridge for 1 hour.

4 To assemble, press a heaped tbsp of rice mixture into one hand, forming a pocket with your palm. Add a generous amount of the beef mixture and a few mozzarella pieces in the middle. Add another scoop of rice on top and form into a ball by pressing on top and bottom. Place on a baking (parchment) paper-lined tray. Repeat with remaining rice and beef mixtures and mozzarella. Chill in the fridge overnight, or at least 1–2 hours.

5 To coat, whisk the eggs in a bowl. Pour the breadcrumbs into a second bowl. One at a time, dip a ball in the egg mix, then roll in the breadcrumbs. Place on a baking (parchment) paper-lined tray.

6 Pour a generous amount of sunflower oil into a saucepan and heat until it reaches 180°C (360°F) or small bubbles appear around the handle of a wooden spoon. Add a few balls at a time, making sure they have room to move around. Fry for 5–7 minutes, or until golden brown and the cheese inside is melted. While you won't be able to see this, it is your role to taste test and make sure they're cooked through!

VINCENZO'S TIPS
- The rice should be dry, al dente rice – not creamy in texture (like risotto).
- Before shaping the arancini, give your hands a quick dip in a bowl of water. It keeps things smooth.
- Let the formed arancini rest to allow the starch in the rice to set, so they don't fall apart when frying.

PIPI ARRUSTUTI ROASTED CAPSICUMS

A staple in Italian cooking, capsicums are so versatile they can be served as part of a salad, side dish or in a stew. Traditionally in Calabria they are prepared with potatoes and olives, and in Nonna Igea's kitchen she sometimes uses one capsicum strip to sweeten her sauce.

Growing up, my family served them roasted, peeled and drenched in extra virgin olive oil at every single barbecue – which, in Australia, is quite often. If you've never tried them this way, make double – they shrink once prepared and are eaten up fast. Vincenzo and I normally rely on my dad to make this vegetarian dish as he is the one typically in charge of the family barbecue, but you can easily grill them using the oven grill (broiler) too. Once they are lavishly drenched in EVOO and mixed with garlic and parsley I cannot think of a better way to eat them than stuffed in a panino, used as a bruschetta topping with slices of salty Pecorino or served alongside a tender piece of steak. Mouth watering yet?

SERVES 4–6
6 capsicums (bell peppers)
extra virgin olive oil (EVOO), qb
3 garlic cloves, diced
bunch of flat-leaf (Italian) parsley, leaves chopped
salt and pepper

METHOD

1 Preheat the oven grill (broiler) to 200°C (390°F). Alternatively, you can use a barbecue grill plate on medium-high.

2 Place the capsicums on a tray lined with baking (parchment) paper. Place the tray in the centre of the oven and grill, turning occasionally so the sides are evenly cooked, for 30 minutes, or until the capsicums have softened and charred. If using the barbecue, place the capsicums straight onto the hot grill, using tongs to turn them when each side is charred and soft. Poke them with a fork in a few spots to check they are soft and have cooked through.

3 Once the capsicums are cooked, remove from the heat. They will look wrinkly and deflated. Place them inside a clean, sealable plastic bag, seal and allow to cool (this will help you remove the skins much more easily). Once cool enough to handle, peel off the skins, scrape out the seeds and pull off the stems. Lay the capsicums flat and cut into long strips.

4 If serving immediately, add them to a bowl and drench with a generous amount of EVOO, as well as the garlic and parsley. Season with salt and pepper before mixing well. Otherwise these will keep well for up to a week in the fridge in an airtight container. Dress them on the day you plan to serve for optimal freshness.

VINCENZO'S TIPS

- Don't be afraid to use different colours and varieties of capsicums. The cooking method doesn't change but the taste will differ slightly. Red is the sweetest!
- The time it takes to grill the capsicums depends on the heat of the grill. Some ovens are stronger and the capsicums will be ready in 20 minutes, but others could take longer.

ZEPPOLE CALABRESE FRIED DOUGH BALLS

If you've never had savoury zeppole, prepare to be hooked. This family recipe, passed down from my papà, became a legend at our local parish festival. Under the hot sun, he would mix and fry massive batches of dough, earning him the title of 'zeppole king' and guaranteeing an endless supply.

These deep-fried morsels of dough, filled with anchovies or enjoyed plain, are the ultimate celebration staple. They'd always hit the table at the end of the night, a celebratory and welcome interruption to the end of a meal when you thought you were full. As Vincenzo learned at first taste, it's impossible to stop at just one. It's not just a recipe, it's a family legacy and a total obsession.

MAKES 30–40

2kg (70.5 oz) plain (all-purpose) flour
1 tbsp white sugar
2 tbsp salt
800ml (27 fl oz) lukewarm water
2 sachets (14g/0.5 oz) dry yeast
sunflower oil, for deep-frying
anchovies or sardines, halved cherry tomatoes or cubed mozzarella, for filling (optional)

METHOD

1 Place the flour, sugar and salt in a large bowl. In a separate bowl, mix the warm water and yeast, dissolving using your hands, then pour into the bowl of flour mixture. Combine using your hands until the dry flour has disappeared into a soft and sticky dough.

2 Once the dough is ready, lay a clean tea towel dampened with cold water over the top. Leave to rest for at least 3 hours at room temperature. You can keep the dough in the fridge, tightly covered in plastic wrap, for up to 3 days. Take out of the fridge 3 hours before frying.

3 Once the dough has risen, pour a generous amount of oil into a deep-fryer or saucepan and heat until it reaches 180°C (360°F) or small bubbles appear around the handle of a wooden spoon. Place a small bowl with cold oil next to you to dip your hands into. Line a tray with paper towel. Prepare your desired fillings on plates next to the large bowl of dough.

4 Remove the cover from the dough and moisten the tips of your fingers and palms using the cold oil (not too much, just slightly). If using anchovies or sardines, like Papà Franco, you can place a few on top of the dough in preparation.

5 Pick up dough where an anchovy is sitting (see images opposite). Fold together, twisting both ends gently (but quickly) to encase the anchovy. Make sure there are no holes and dough is not too thin. If using tomatoes or mozzarella, keep dough thick enough to prevent bursting and oil seepage. You don't need fillings – we also love them plain!

6 Drop the filled zeppole into the hot oil, then make and add a few more without overcrowding, so the oil temperature doesn't drop too quickly. Move each one around gently with tongs, making sure it is well cooked on the outside and through the centre. You may need to turn them a few times. Once completely golden, transfer to prepared tray to drain. Test the first one is cooked through by breaking in half. Serve immediately.

PAPÀ FRANCO'S TIPS

- To make a smaller number of zeppole, use 1kg (35 oz) flour and half the quantity of the other dough ingredients.
- To speed up activating the yeast, keep the bowl in a warm environment.
- Getting the right size zeppole might require some trial and error. Make a few and adjust how much dough you pick up if you want them smaller or bigger.
- Enlist the help of a volunteer to turn the zeppole if you don't want to get your tongs messy.

FRITTATA DI SPINACI SPINACH FRITTATA

Vincenzo loves making his nonna's spinach frittata for a quick, nutritious meal that the whole family loves – well, everyone, except our eldest, Sebastian, who was obsessed with it yesterday and refuses to touch it today. Ah, toddler life!

When we were dating, Vincenzo introduced me to this classic and seriously underrated Italian dish. I had no idea that the 'real' version was just eggs and vegetables – I honestly thought he'd made a mistake. Oops!

This recipe shines when we use fresh, organic eggs, preferably from Nonna Igea's local farmer in Italy. But when that's not possible, we've found the secret to a perfect frittata is adding an extra egg and not skimping on the cheese. Nonna Igea serves it as a secondo on top of fresh Italian bread. We often have it for breakfast – just don't tell Vincenzo's family, who prefer their sweet cornetto pastries!

SERVES 4 AS A SIDE

1 tbsp extra virgin olive oil (EVOO), plus extra, for drizzling
5 cups (150g/5.3 oz) baby spinach
6 eggs
salt and pepper
3 tbsp finely grated Pecorino Romano, plus extra to serve (optional)
130ml (4.4 fl oz) full cream milk
small bunch of flat-leaf (Italian) parsley, leaves finely chopped (optional)
pane di casa or sourdough, to serve

METHOD

1 Preheat the oven to 180°C (360°F).

2 Heat the EVOO in a non-stick ovenproof skillet over medium heat, then add the spinach. Cook, covered, for 2–3 minutes, stirring occasionally. If it dries out, add a bit of extra oil or water. Once wilted, remove from heat and transfer to a bowl.

3 Crack the eggs into a large bowl and season with a pinch of salt and a generous amount of pepper. Whisk well. Add the Pecorino, milk and parsley, then whisk again.

4 Add the cooked spinach once cooled and use a fork to break down the leaves and combine.

5 Return pan to medium-high heat. Drizzle in extra EVOO to line the pan. Wipe the excess with paper towel, making sure it's spread all over. Once warm, pour in the mixture. Wait for 2–4 minutes, or until bubbles begin to form around the edge. Don't touch the frittata; it will continue to bubble while it cooks underneath and starts to heat through.

6 Once the top and edge of the frittata begin to cook but still appear runny, transfer the pan to the oven for 10 minutes, or until the top has cooked through and started to rise.

7 Remove the pan from the oven (remember to cover the handle with a dry tea towel or oven mitt as it will be hot!). Place a large plate on top of the pan, then carefully flip the frittata onto the plate. Return it to the pan, cooked-side up, and cook for 1–2 minutes over medium heat (or back in the oven) to finish.

8 Grate extra Pecorino on top, if using, while the frittata is hot, to melt. (Vincenzo always adds more cheese, of course!) Slice into triangles and serve on crusty Italian bread.

VINCENZO'S TIPS

- The milk makes the frittata moist and creamy. Some people prefer to use cream instead of milk, but as I've always said, 'Milk is a natural cream', and there's no need to ever use cream!
- Make sure your skillet is hot before pouring the frittata mixture into it. This will help stabilise the bottom of the frittata and make the edge cook immediately.

SAUCES

SAUCES

Welcome to the heart of flavour. In Italian cuisine, sauces aren't just an afterthought – they're the cornerstone of many classic dishes. This is where the magic happens, where simple ingredients transform into something extraordinary. It's our goal to fill your senses with the kind of comforting aromas that transport you directly to Nonna Igea's kitchen, where she stirs a bubbling pot of sugo or has just picked basil from her garden for a batch of homemade pesto.

Vincenzo's family is close-knit, all living in the same four-storey building that Nonno Angelo built with his own hands. It was common in Italian culture for families to stay near one another, and the structure Nonno built ensured that his growing family could do just that. Vincenzo's mum and dad live at the top, his two uncles in between, while Nonna holds court at the bottom, filling the whole building with her cooking. No matter what's on her cooktop, the delicious scents travel upward. But when it's her sugo, as soon as we open the door, we call down via the internal intercom to Nonna's place and ask if we can join her for a meal. She always responds with a warm laugh and a joyful, 'Ma certo, c'è sempre cibo per tutti (But of course, there's always enough food for everyone'), as if the thought of us not going would never have entered her mind.

The beauty of these sauces is in their simplicity. From rich, hearty passata to delicate and aromatic pesto and the most authentic bolognese, this chapter is short, but its pages are filled with the soul of Italian cooking. Each recipe holds a story, a tradition and a sense of nostalgia. Your family might have their own secret ingredient for a classic sauce, or you might have picked up a trick or two from a trip to Italy or a cooking class with Vincenzo. These sauces are the unsung heroes of countless meals, the key to recreating unforgettable flavours passed down through generations. Because when the sauce is right, everything else falls into place.

SUGO DI POMODORO E BASILICO — TOMATO AND BASIL SAUCE

Every family has their own twist on this beloved, household staple (and, of course, my family's version and Vincenzo's are not quite identical). Some opt for the boldness of onions, while others swear by the aromatic allure of garlic. But for us, simplicity reigns supreme. Inspired by the teachings of Nonna Igea, Vincenzo crafted a fresh interpretation that has become the beating heart of our kitchen. The base (soffritto) is made up of blended carrot, celery and onion. Combine this with homemade tomato passata and the delicate fragrance of fresh basil, and you've created a vibrant sugo that can be used in a variety of dishes, whether dancing between a mound of spaghetti, scooped up with crusty Italian bread, or as the base for cannelloni (see recipe, page 117).

2.5/3L OR 10/12 CUPS (ALLOWS EXTRA TO STORE)
1 carrot, roughly chopped
½ medium-sized brown onion, roughly chopped
1 celery stalk
extra virgin olive oil (EVOO), qb
2.5kg (88 oz) canned peeled Italian tomatoes, or store-bought passatta or use homemade (see recipe, page 74)
2 tsp rock salt
freshly cracked black pepper
75–100g (2.6–3.5 oz) fresh basil leaves, plus extra to serve
your choice of pasta shape, rock salt and finely grated Pecorino Romano, to serve

SPECIAL EQUIPMENT
blender

METHOD

1 For the soffritto, blend the carrot, onion, celery, and about 3 tbsp EVOO and 1 splash of water until thick and creamy – like a velvety purée!

2 Add 3–4 tbsp of EVOO and 1 tbsp of water to a pot, then pour in the soffritto. Place on low heat, stirring gently to cover the base. Cover with a lid and simmer, stirring often with a wooden spoon to prevent burning, for 7–10 minutes, or until it glistens and the vegetables become tender.

3 Meanwhile, if you are using chopped or peeled tomatoes, blend them so they break down and create a thick consistency.

4 When the soffritto is ready, mix the passata (or blended tomatoes) through and combine using a wooden spoon. Sprinkle in rock salt and a pinch of black pepper, then mix through. Cover and simmer on low heat for 1 hour, stirring occasionally. Remove the lid and simmer for another 30–45 minutes, or until it thickens to your preference. Turn off the heat. Tear the basil and add it to the sauce while still hot, allowing it to infuse.

5 Bring a large pot of water to a rolling boil, add rock salt, allow to dissolve and then cook your pasta according to packet instructions. Once al dente, reserve ½ mug pasta water then drain the pasta. In a separate pan on medium-low heat, add a ladle or two of sugo, then add the pasta with a splash of pasta water, and toss to thicken. Add another ladle or two of sugo to your preference in the pan and toss again, adding more pasta water only if needed. To garnish alla Vincenzo, sprinkle with grated Pecorino (or Parmigiano) and fresh basil.

VINCENZO'S TIPS
- Source only the highest quality passata or canned tomatoes. In this case, Italian is best. If you can't, you might want to hunt down the freshest, farm-grown tomatoes you can and make your own passata.
- The basil leaves are only to be added at the end, capisci? If they're cooked too long, they'll lose their fragrant charm.
- Freeze leftover sugo for up to 6 months in clean, airtight mason jars (just don't overfill). To thaw, place in the fridge overnight or in a bowl of hot water. Once the sugo starts to melt, pour it into a pan and heat gently.

RAGÙ ALLA BOLOGNESE BOLOGNESE SAUCE

This isn't the bolognese you think you know. My opinion of this classic was forever changed in Bologna, thanks to Vincenzo. We discovered the soul of this dish after tasting it in only the most authentic trattorias, and devouring a trusted recipe from our good friend David's nonna, who shared this rich, velvety masterpiece that is a true act of love. Forget every bland, rushed version you've ever tried. A real bolognese is a five-hour commitment, simmered low and slow. This recipe is our promise that patience is the most powerful ingredient when making an authentic ragù, proving that anything less would be a betrayal of true Italian cuisine (and might make Vincenzo shed a tear).

SERVES 6 (FREEZE LEFTOVERS FOR UP TO 6 MONTHS)

extra virgin olive oil (EVOO), qb
1 red or brown onion, diced
3 carrots, diced
3 celery stalks, diced
1 glass red wine
500g (17.6 oz) minced (ground) pork
300g (10.6 oz) minced (ground) beef
200g (7 oz) minced (ground) veal
salt and pepper, qb
4 cups (1L/33.75 fl oz) store-bought passata or use homemade (see recipe, page 74)
150g (5.3 oz) concentrated tomato paste
400g (14.1 oz) canned peeled Italian tomatoes
4 cups (1L/33.75 fl oz) boiling water
1 cup (250 ml/8.5 fl oz) full cream milk
tagliatelle or pappardelle pasta, rock salt and finely grated Parmigiano Reggiano or Pecorino Romano, to serve

METHOD

1 For the soffritto, heat a generous amount of EVOO in a large saucepan over medium heat. Once hot, add the onion. When it turns glossy and golden, add the carrot and celery. Cook, stirring occasionally, for 4–5 minutes.

2 Add half the wine and simmer over low heat, stirring every so often, for 2–3 minutes, or until the wine almost evaporates. Add the minces, breaking them up with a wooden spoon, then season with salt and pepper. Stir occasionally to cook through, allowing to brown lightly. Once the mince dries out, add the remaining wine and simmer until it evaporates. Stir in the passata, tomato paste and peeled tomatoes, crushing the tomatoes with the spoon. Simmer, uncovered, for 1½ hours, stirring every 20 minutes.

3 Pour in the boiling water and mix through. Taste for salt and adjust if needed. Cook, uncovered, for 1 more hour, stirring occasionally, and if it looks dry, add ½ cup water at a time. Keep it to a gentle simmer; if it is bubbling too much, reduce the heat. Simmer for another 2½ hours, keeping the pot uncovered the whole time.

4 Stir through the milk. This traditional step softens the acidity of the tomatoes and gives the sauce its creamy texture – don't skip it! (Please don't substitute cream for the milk – you'll hear Vincenzo's cries in your kitchen if you do!) Simmer, stirring occasionally, for 5 minutes then turn off the heat.

5 Bring a large pot of water to a rolling boil, add rock salt, allow to dissolve and then cook your pasta according to packet instructions. Once al dente, reserve 1 mug of pasta water then drain the pasta.

6 In a frying pan over low heat, add a generous ladle of sauce to cover the base. Add the pasta and a splash of the reserved pasta water, mixing until the strands of pasta are smothered by the sauce. Add more sauce if desired, then toss to emulsify. Serve topped with cheese.

DAVID'S TIPS
- There is no need to add herbs; carrot, onion and celery provide enough flavour.
- Cook this sauce, uncovered, for no less than 5 hours. Tempted to cook it for less than that? Don't do it! Every hour makes a difference.
- Season the sauce gradually throughout cooking. Start with a small amount of salt and adjust as needed towards the end. This approach helps you avoid over-salting, as flavours can become more concentrated over time.

PESTO AL BASILICO BASIL PESTO

Confession: in our early years dating I once served store-bought pesto to Vincenzo. I know, I know, how could I? But I had to start somewhere. In a pinch, even the best cooks need an 'emergency pesto'. These days, I'm a full-on pesto purist. No cream (Vincenzo would faint!), just the essentials: fresh basil, pine nuts, garlic, Parmigiano and a good splash of extra virgin olive oil. A mortar and pestle is ideal for that rustic charm, but we often reach for the food processor – follow Vincenzo's method to avoid overheating the basil and keep it from turning bitter. It's a game-changer.

Homemade pesto is pure magic over pasta, grilled chicken or lamb, but my favourite pairing? With homemade gnocchi (see recipes, pages 92, 95). Making pesto with Nonna is another kind of magic. More cheese? Of course. Extra pine nuts? Absolutely. We may argue about the perfect balance, but the laughter, and the incredible aroma we undoutedly create, makes every spoonful of this dish worth it.

MAKES ABOUT 250G (SERVES 2)
1 cup loosely packed (20g/0.7 oz) basil leaves, washed, plus extra if needed
1/3 cup (80ml/2.7 fl oz) extra virgin olive oil (EVOO), plus extra, qb
1 garlic clove
20g (0.7 oz) pine nuts (toasted optional)
4 tbsp (2 oz) finely grated Parmigiano Reggiano or Pecorino Romano, plus extra if needed
your choice of pasta shape, to serve

SPECIAL EQUIPMENT
blender, or mortar and pestle

METHOD

1 To absorb excess water from washing the basil, place a paper towel on top of the leaves and press down gently. Repeat until almost completely dry.

2 Place 50ml (1.7 fl oz) (a little less or more will work too) of EVOO in a blender or food processor, then the garlic. Blend for 1 minute, or until you get a smooth, creamy consistency. Add the pine nuts, then blend again. Next add the basil, cheese and 2 tbsp EVOO and blend, using the pulse setting only, for 30 seconds. This is important because you don't want to overheat and oxidise the basil. If after this time there is still cheese around the edge, scrape it back in, mix using a tablespoon or spatula and pulse again until combined.

4 Using a small spoon (or your finger – but switch off the blender first!), taste the pesto for salt and flavour – if it is too salty, add extra basil leaves and a drop of EVOO. Not enough flavour? Add more cheese. Pulse blend until you reach your perfect consistency.

5 To serve pesto with your pasta, you don't need to cook it before combining the two. Simply add it to a large pan pan over low heat, warm it gently for 1–2 minutes, then mix it with your cooked pasta, adding a splash of pasta water as you toss it together to help cover all your pasta. This will ensure you keep the flavours strong and prevent the pesto from drying out.

VINCENZO'S TIPS
- Store the pesto in a tightly sealed jar in the fridge and add a drizzle of EVOO on top after each time you eat some, to keep out air and prevent mould. This keeps it fresh … if it even lasts that long!
- For single servings, double the recipe and portion into ice cube trays, for easy, year-long freezer storage. Use about a quarter of the doubled recipe per serving.
- You know I would substitute in Pecorino, but while this is acceptable to Italians, it will be saltier, so add a small amount at a time rather than all at once.
- Never 'cook' the pesto; warm it gently for a couple of minutes at most to keep those flavours bright.

BESCIAMELLA BÉCHAMEL SAUCE

In Italy, it's called besciamella, a creamy sauce made from butter, flour and milk, and it is the secret to making a great lasagna, pasta al forno, cannelloni and lots of other baked dishes. It's the only kind of cream Vincenzo will advocate for (savoury at least, sweet is another story!) and once you taste it, you'll understand why.

While it's believed that béchamel originated in France, some say it actually comes from Tuscany. Regardless of its roots, this sauce has found a home in Italian kitchens. Aside from helping to bond pasta or crepes, you can also pour it over cooked, sliced potatoes or other grilled or roasted vegetables for a delicious, simple side dish. The key to making besciamella is to get the measurements and the timing spot on. This recipe is a great guide for that. If you master this sauce, you'll have a foundation for many Italian favourites.

MAKES ENOUGH FOR 1 LASAGNA
25g (0.9 oz) butter
25g (0.9 oz) plain (all-purpose) flour
1 cup (250ml/8.4 fl oz) full cream milk
sprinkle of nutmeg (freshly grated or ground)
salt and pepper

METHOD

1 Place a small saucepan over low heat, add the butter and let it slowly, gently melt.

2 Begin adding the flour, whisking constantly until it disappears and the mixture becomes creamy, and lump-free. Don't let it brown.

3 Add half the milk to the pan. Increase the heat to medium–low and whisk gently but swiftly. As the sauce thickens, add more milk and continue to stir. Don't add the milk too quickly or it will start to form clumps that can be hard to get rid of. Don't allow the sauce to dry out, just add a portion at a time and stir.

4 When the sauce has achieved your desired consistency (see tip below), turn off the heat and stop stirring, making sure there are no lumps from the flour and that it has fully melted into the butter and milk. Quickly remove from the heat.

5 Add a sprinkle of nutmeg to enhance the flavour (if using fresh, add less), along with a pinch of salt and pepper and mix through. Use the besciamella while warm on your favourite dish of choice.

VINCENZO'S TIPS
- Don't rush! If you turn up the heat to melt the butter faster, it'll brown and ruin the base – patience is key.
- When whisking, make sure you don't walk away – creating the right consistency is key, or else you will need to start over.
- When it comes to the consistency of the sauce in step 4, for lasagna you'll want to make it thinner and easier to pour and spread. For other baked dishes, a thicker texture is what you'll be looking for.

SUGO ALLA MARINARA MARINARA SAUCE

When Vincenzo was asked to share the true marinara, it set him on a mission to make it (you guessed it) authentically and serve it at home. Known also as Neapolitan sauce, this hails from Naples, where the locals one day decided to try their pizza sauce on pasta. It soon became the most popular Italian sauce in existence. With just three essential ingredients – Italian peeled tomatoes, garlic and oregano – and a little over 10 minutes of cooking time, it will transform your kitchen into a fragrant homage to Nonna's own. Next time you are at the supermarket, compare these ingredients to those on a jar of marinara. Then, buy the ones listed here, go home and jar your own.

SERVES 4–5
800g (28.2 oz) canned whole peeled Italian tomatoes
extra virgin olive oil (EVOO), qb
4 garlic cloves, crushed
3 oregano sprigs, leaves picked, stems discarded
salt and pepper
pinch or two of chilli flakes, to taste (optional)
small handful basil leaves, roughly torn (optional)
spaghetti, or your choice of pasta shape, and
  finely grated Pecorino Romano or Parmigiano
  Reggiano, to serve

METHOD

1 Pour the tomatoes into a bowl and crush them with a potato masher or your hands until until mostly smooth, leaving some small chunks for texture.

2 Warm 5 tbsp EVOO in a saucepan over medium heat. Add the garlic, spreading it with a wooden spoon. Add a splash of water to prevent the garlic from burning. Once the garlic starts to turn lightly golden, add the crushed tomatoes and squash them down with the spoon. When the sauce starts to simmer, stir in most of the oregano, as well as a pinch of salt and pepper, and chilli, if using. Cook uncovered over low heat, stirring occasionally, for up to 20 minutes.

3 Meanwhile, bring a large pot of water to a rolling boil, add rock salt, allow to dissolve and then cook your pasta according to packet instructions. Once al dente, reserve ½ mug pasta water then drain the pasta.

4 Remove sauce from the heat, stir in most of the basil, if using, and remaining oregano. Add the pasta directly to the pan of sauce, tossing to combine. Use the reserved pasta water as needed to loosen and help thicken, then plate and top with remaining basil and cheese.

VINCENZO'S TIPS
- This is rustic at its best. Don't attempt to break down every single piece of tomato – small chunks will add a beautiful texture.
- Fresh oregano is worth the effort – it's affordable and far better than dried. If using dried, add sparingly and taste as you go to avoid overpowering the dish.
- The sauce should not be watery or runny. If you feel it is watery for any reason, cook it a little longer over low heat.

SALSA DI POMODORO PER LA PIZZA   TOMATO SAUCE FOR PIZZA

If you have mastered (or even attempted to make) homemade pizza dough, there is no way you should settle for a store-bought pizza sauce. It can be a minefield – too salty, too bitter or just plain wrong. Picture Vincenzo's expression at the thought of it and you'll be turned off!

For Vincenzo – and most Italians – pizza isn't simply another food; it's an entire food group and a sacred tradition. There are rituals around crafting the perfect dough, and one thing often taken for granted is the sauce, but it is equally as vital!

This recipe was shared with Vincenzo by native-Neapolitan and award-winning pizzaiolo Lucio de Falco. The first time Vincenzo tasted it, he realised it was a pivotal ingredient that completely transformed the pizza experience. This is the authentic taste of Naples, crafted to elevate your homemade pizza to a whole new level. It starts with high-quality peeled tomatoes and just three other ingredients that take only a few minutes to combine – no cooking required. Now, not only will your guests ask for your pizza dough recipe, they'll beg for your pizza sauce one too!

MAKES ENOUGH FOR 6 MEDIUM PIZZAS
800g (28.2 oz) canned peeled Italian tomatoes (San Marzano is preferred)
8g (1½ tsp) salt (see note)
handful of basil leaves, full or torn
extra virgin olive oil (EVOO), for drizzling

METHOD

1 Place the tomatoes in a bowl and crush them with a potato masher or your hands to create a thick, coarse sauce full of tomato pieces. You do this to keep the freshness of the tomatoes and avoid breaking the seeds, which can create a bitter taste.

2 Add the salt and continue to mix with your hands by immersing one hand in the tomatoes and squeezing until the tomatoes are fully crushed. Use your other hand to turn the bowl and make sure it's mixed well.

3 Add the basil and keep mixing. Finally, add a drizzle of EVOO and mix through. Taste once it is ready and adjust seasoning to your preference.

LUCIO'S TIPS
- Season according to your tastebuds, but the golden rule is to use 1g of salt per 100g of tomatoes.
- For a rich, flavourful sauce, make it a day ahead. Letting it rest overnight deepens the taste and infuses the basil flavour.
- Don't ask about a blender! Your hands are the best utensil for crushing tomatoes.
- Never cook your sauce before putting it on a pizza. Ever. Store it in the fridge in a sealed container for up to 4 days. This ensures the flavour of the sauce is as close as possible to eating fresh tomatoes – they cook more than enough once the pizza is in the hot oven.

PASSATA RUSTICA DI POMODORO HOMEMADE TOMATO PASSATA

Making your own passata is like bottling a bit of Italy in your kitchen. Vincenzo's small-batch recipe lets us capture the rich, sweet flavours of homemade sugo without the grand affair of a traditional Passata Day. Still a simple, joyful task, it just doesn't require an entire day or army of helpers. Whenever our pantry stock runs low or a craving for homemade sauce strikes, we whip up a few bottles, knowing exactly what goes into each one. Store-bought passata is easy, sure, but the additives aren't too appealing. Vincenzo likes to say, 'You become what you eat,' so why not make it fresh? It's affordable, tastes far better, and turns cooking into a family event – even if it gets a little messy with the kids in the kitchen.

MAKES 3 × 700ML (70 FL OZ) BOTTLES
5kg (176.4 oz) ripened roma or heirloom tomatoes, washed, trimmed and halved
½ red capsicum (bell pepper), destemmed, deseeded and sliced into thin strips
2 tbsp (1 oz) rock salt
small bunch of basil, washed and dried

SPECIAL EQUIPMENT
3–4 large sterilised glass bottles with lid
rotary food mill or potato ricer
kitchen funnel

METHOD

1 Add the tomato to a large pot. Fill 1 bottle halfway with water, pour this into the pan, then add the capsicum into the pot and mix using your hands.

2 Cook over medium heat, stirring every 5 minutes, for 20–25 minutes, or until the tomato breaks down into a thick consistency and the capsicum has softened. Cook longer, if needed.

3 Place a large colander over a bowl and pour in the tomato mixture. Let the liquid drain, then transfer the liquid to another bowl and strain the tomato again if needed. Repeat until the tomato is free of excess liquid.

4 Spoon some of the tomato mixture into a food mill or potato ricer set over a large bowl and pass it through using the small setting – this keeps the skin from slipping through while letting the smooth tomato purée drop into the bowl. Once done, set aside the tomato skins.

5 Repeat until you have passed all the tomato mixture through. Occasionally, scrape down the bottom of the mill or ricer and let the pulp fall into the bowl.

6 Pass the skins and flesh through again, then add salt to the pulp and mix until dissolved.

7 Add a few basil leaves to the bottom of each sterilised bottle, then use a funnel to pour in the passata until each bottle is just over three-quarters full. Seal tightly using only new lids. Place the bottles in a large saucepan, cover with water and boil for 20 minutes to seal. Leave to cool down, then remove the bottles from the water and store.

VINCENZO'S TIPS

- No food mill or potato ricer? No problem! Use a food processor and strain the purée through a fine sieve.
- If you don't like the consistency with the seeds, you are best to use a food mill and ensure you are only choosing the smallest setting. Any other utensil will not prevent the seeds from falling in.
- The strained tomato liquid can be bitter, but don't throw it out. It's great for vegetable stock or adding flavour to soups and sauces. Nonna would approve – nothing goes to waste!
- Once sealed, store the bottles in a cool, dark place. My nonni had a whole shelf of them in their garage! They're fine without refrigeration until opened and can last a year or longer if sealed right. For long-term storage, it can help to add a thin layer of EVOO on top of the passata in each bottle.

FRESH PASTA

FRESH PASTA

This chapter is a love story. It's where it all started – Nonna Igea's passion, Vincenzo's inspiration and the affection we all have for one of Italy's oldest rituals: pasta making.

These pages are filled with luscious strands of silky pasta, thick traditional chitarra, scrumptious ravioli, and Vincenzo's ricotta gnocchi. We start with Nonna's original egg pasta dough recipe, easily recreated with a rolling pin or pasta machine. Vincenzo has watched his nonna make pasta dough countless times and yet every time she does, it's like we all see it for the first time. I feel like we blink and suddenly there is a golden ball of pasta dough ready to be transformed into something spectacular. She makes it look so effortless and yet it feels a little intimidating.

'My hands have been doing this for many years,' she always tells me. 'They have been making pasta since I was 12 years old. One day you'll be fast too, but for now, just practise.'

I can proudly say we have practised many times with her keen eyes watching over us and it always ends the same way. When we check in with her she proceeds to give it a final knead and help it take shape, and with that one swift motion the dough becomes utter perfection. 'Hai fatto un buon lavoro. La prossima volta, lo farai ancora meglio (You did a good job. Next time it will be better still),' she says, and I smirk because I know there is no way I'll ever get the final touch when we're together. But honestly, it's OK with me. Nothing comes close to her pasta.

What you need to keep in mind when making pasta is to trust in the process. You might be mid-kneading and think it won't turn out, but it will – and if it's a little dry or a little moist there are tricks to get it back on track. Imagine Nonna reminding you that it all comes with experience. The more you make it, the better it will turn out.

PASTA ALL'UOVO FRESH EGG PASTA DOUGH

Nonna Igea's egg pasta dough recipe is fool-proof. Two ingredients and your hands are all it takes to make the base and then you can let your creativity take over when deciding what shape of pasta you will be rolling out and the dish you'll create.

Nonna catered a wedding reception at the age of 12 and it started with eggs and flour. She made pasta and fed the whole town, quickly becoming known as a young master in the art. If anyone should be teaching us the techniques for making pasta dough, it is her. She is now almost 90 and still very much a perfectionist, feeding pasta to the masses and getting it right. Every. Single. Time. So if you're considering making pasta from scratch, follow this recipe and channel Nonna – she'll be by your side every step of the way and you will be so proud when you sit down to eat the final dish.

SERVES 1+
100g (3.5 oz) plain (all-purpose) or tipo '00' flour per serving, plus extra for kneading
1 egg per serving

SPECIAL EQUIPMENT
rolling pin or pasta machine

METHOD

1 Measure 100g (3.5 oz) flour per person and 1 egg each. Nonna stands by this amount every time (although she doesn't need a scale as she's capable of measuring the exact amount of flour with the palm of her hand!).

2 Create a mound with the flour on your bench then put all your fingers together into a point on one hand and, using your fingertips, make a small well in the middle. Crack the eggs into the well and whisk using a fork or your hands (Nonna would use her hands, so try it). Slowly pull the flour from the side of the well into the egg, mixing it through, being careful not to let the egg escape! Once it's combined, mix any excess flour left on your board through too. Then, start to press down and forward on the dough with the palm of your hands, then fold back in with your fingers and repeat. Knead the dough using this method for at least 10 minutes or until it smooths out and softens in consistency.

3 Once it's smooth and has softened, create a ball and cover it tightly with plastic wrap or a large bowl placed upside down. Leave to rest for 20 minutes.

4 Remove the plastic wrap or bowl, cut a thick piece, and cover the remaining dough again to keep it from drying out. Press down with your hands on the piece you've cut to flatten it slightly. Sprinkle flour on top, and roll it out, first forward then back, with your rolling pin. Turn the dough around, rolling out the thicker parts a few times to make it even and smooth. Repeat until all the dough is used. As you go, keep the sheets covered with a tea towel so they don't dry out.

5 You can roll out lasagna sheets and cut them to size using this method; or use a sharp knife to cut the sheets into strands of pasta to your chosen thickness. Below, we've given instructions for making pappardelle and tagliatelle by hand, and for making spaghetti, fettuccine and lasagna using a pasta machine.

FOR PAPPARDELLE BY HAND

Pappardelle, originally from Tuscany, are large and quite broad. They're often the base of hearty meals paired with a rich, meaty ragù such as our Wild boar ragù (see recipe, page 138).

If you've never tried this pasta, get ready to become something of an egg pasta snob. We're convinced you will never look back, so don't try it if you want to stay in the pasta comfort zone. It all likely boils down to the origin of the name, which comes from the Italian verb *pappare*, which means 'to gobble up'! So, if you find yourself feasting on more than you might have expected, don't stop – just remember, that's the intention of this pasta! You can then justify this by saying, 'The pasta made me do it', because by definition, it in fact did.

Pappardelle are best cut by hand rather than a pasta machine. To make:

1 Follow steps 1–6 here to roll out your pasta sheets, then sprinkle flour on your board. Place a pasta sheet on top, dusting both sides with flour. Fold this in half, then fold it in half again and, finally, one last time.

2 Using a sharp knife or pastry cutter, slice strands approximately 2–3cm (1 inch) apart until you have cut up the entire sheet, then unravel them to reveal the strands of pappardelle – each piece you cut will be a strip of pasta. Repeat for each pasta sheet.

NONNA IGEA'S TIPS
- The size of the well you create before adding the eggs is determined by how many you need to add. Keep it slightly deep to prevent the egg from flowing out.
- When you start to combine the flour and egg, you might notice it isn't coming together, but just keep going – the process takes time, patience and trust!
- If the dough feels a bit dry once you have been kneading for a little while, wet your hands slightly and continue to knead. Avoid adding water as this will change the consistency of the dough.
- Use high-quality flour to make the dough. Semolina is a popular choice for pappardelle, but it will be harder in texture and likely take longer to cook.
- Use your hands and not a stand mixer to combine the flour and egg – and no need for salt, no matter what anyone on the internet says! Salt is added to the water when you cook your pasta. While I'm at it, please don't add oil when you boil the pasta. It is of no use.
- Instead of straining using a colander, remove fresh pasta with tongs, because flour from the pasta can settle at the bottom of the pot. Be gentle! Fresh pasta can break easily.

PASTA ALL'UOVO FRESH EGG PASTA DOUGH (CONT'D)

FOR TAGLIATELLE BY HAND

Fresh egg tagliatelle are so versatile. If you like longer, thin strands of pasta but with a little width, these might be your new favourite. They are flat in shape and while delicious with bold sauces, they also pair well with vegetables and seafood. We like to use them when we can't decide what pasta to serve, mainly because they go with everything. Naturally they are *the* choice for traditional bolognese, and once you make the switch from spaghetti you will finally understand what Vincenzo is always whining about!

These can be cut by hand or you can use your pasta machine if you have the correct setting.

1 Follow steps 1–5 on page 80 to roll out your pasta sheets, sprinkle flour on your board and place a pasta sheet on top, then dust both sides lightly with flour. Carefully fold your pasta sheet in half. Continue folding it in half several times until you have a compact strip of dough about 3cm (1¼ inch) wide. Repeat with remaining pasta sheets.

2 Cut each strip into pieces using a pastry cutter or sharp knife, measuring about 1.5cm (0.59 inch) between each cut, then unravel them to reveal the strands of tagliatelle.

For the ultimate dish, make a slow-cooked Bolognese ragù (see recipe, page 63). Serve with grated Parmigiano or Pecorino.

ROLLING THE PASTA USING A PASTA MACHINE

1 Cut a piece of dough and sprinkle flour on top. Once you have assembled and secured the pasta machine, sprinkle some flour on top of the section where you push the pasta through. Turn the dial to the widest setting.

2 Press down on the dough before passing it through the machine on its side so it's wide, not thin and long. Once it has come through, fold it over and pass through again, then one more time without folding.

3 Move on to the consecutive settings, and continue until you reach the desired thickness, which all depends on the pasta shape you want to make. Typically pasta machines come with spaghetti, fettuccine and a wide setting for pasta sheets.

4 Once you have chosen your shape, add more flour to the dough and the machine and pass it through. Don't leave the sheets long; cut them in half instead so your pasta doesn't end up as extra long strands. If it does, simply slice the strands in half before storing or cooking.

HOW TO STORE PASTA

Either store the pasta flat or create pasta nests by unraveling the pasta gently and sprinkling some flour on top, before twisting together to create small nests. Dust a tray with flour then place the pasta or nests on top and leave them to rest for 24 hours in the fridge, or freeze them. After they have frozen on the tray, you can transfer them to tightly sealed containers to maintain their freshness. Use within 6 months.

HOW TO COOK AND SERVE

Depending on your homemade pasta shape, choose a recipe from the Sauces chapter (see pages 60–74) or the Primi chapter (see pages 100–58) to cook up a luscious, homemade pasta dish.

Pasta made with fresh dough hits differently. There are some recipes Vincenzo doesn't love to serve with it because it might make the final dish too heavy, but in all honesty, to really test how good your fresh pasta is, start by serving it with a Tomato and basil sugo (see recipe, page 60) or Pesto (see recipe, page 64).

To cook, bring a large pot of water to boil, add 1 tbsp rock salt, and add the pasta. Cook for 4–6 minutes (depending on the thickness; if thin, even less) then remove with tongs and combine with your sauce. If cooking from frozen, don't defrost it – cook right away and for an extra 1–2 minutes. Either way, do a taste test in between and aim for al dente.

PASTA VERDE AGLI SPINACI SPINACH PASTA

Green pasta? Why not! Infuse your pasta dough with spinach and add a whole new element of flavour to your meal. Not to mention vibrancy. By adding just one extra ingredient, your pasta dough will be completely transformed – and you'll sneak in a few extra vitamins and minerals while you're at it too.

SERVES 2–4
150g (5.3 oz) fresh spinach (baby spinach can also be used)
sprinkle of salt
250g (8.8 oz) plain (all purpose) or tipo '00' flour, plus extra, for dusting
2 eggs

SPECIAL EQUIPMENT
food processor or blender
rolling pin or pasta machine

METHOD

1 Place the spinach in a pan on medium heat. Sprinkle with a pinch of salt and cook for 2–3 minutes, stirring occasionally with a wooden spoon so it doesn't stick to the bottom. Add a splash of water if necessary to avoid it drying up. Once wilted, it is cooked. Squeeze out any water, then add the spinach to a food processor, and blend until creamy. Set aside to cool.

2 To make the pasta, create a mound with the flour on the bench. Make a well in the centre using your fingers, then add the eggs and 1 heaped tbsp of spinach cream. Using a fork, whisk the eggs with the spinach and slowly mix the flour by pulling the sides of the well in gently first. Once the spinach and egg have disappeared into the flour, use your hands to combine the rest of the flour and bring it all together, then knead the dough for 15–20 minutes. Knead by folding it, then press down with a forward motion and repeat. This helps mix everything together well and will create the perfect texture.

3 When the consistency is smooth, even if there is leftover flour on the bench, scrape it to the side. If, however, it is still sticky, knead using an extra dusting of flour. Once ready, create a ball and wrap it tightly in plastic wrap. Set aside for 30 minutes.

4 After the dough has rested, sprinkle flour over your bench, unwrap the dough and dust some extra flour on top. Roll out your pasta to your desired shape following the instructions on page 80 (Vincenzo adores using this pasta to make tagliatelle or fettuccine, but you could make any variety you like – even ravioli or lasagna). Keep unused pasta dough covered to prevent it drying out.

5 To cook fresh or from frozen, follow the directions on page 83 and serve with your favourite sauce. Alternatively, this pasta is full of flavour on its own, so you could drizzle some EVOO (or some melted butter) on top once cooked, along with some pasta water, toss it through and add a few dollops of fresh ricotta or stracciatella cheese, and a drizzle of EVOO (don't forget the Pecorino).

VINCENZO'S TIPS

- Use fresh spinach that's bright green and crisp. Don't wait a few days or let it wilt. Frozen is less than ideal due to its water content, but if it is all you have just strain once cooked until there is next to no water left.
- Keep some extra flour close by and sprinkle it over your hands as you knead the dough to get rid of the excess sticky bits that are likely to be all over them!
- Keep any leftover spinach cream in the fridge to spread on a panino with mozzarella, or serve it with lamb cutlets or grilled chicken the following day.
- You can use this method with a variety of vegetables, such as pumpkin or carrot. The one rule to remember, whether using spinach or another vegetable, is to ensure there is as little water in it as possible before kneading it through.

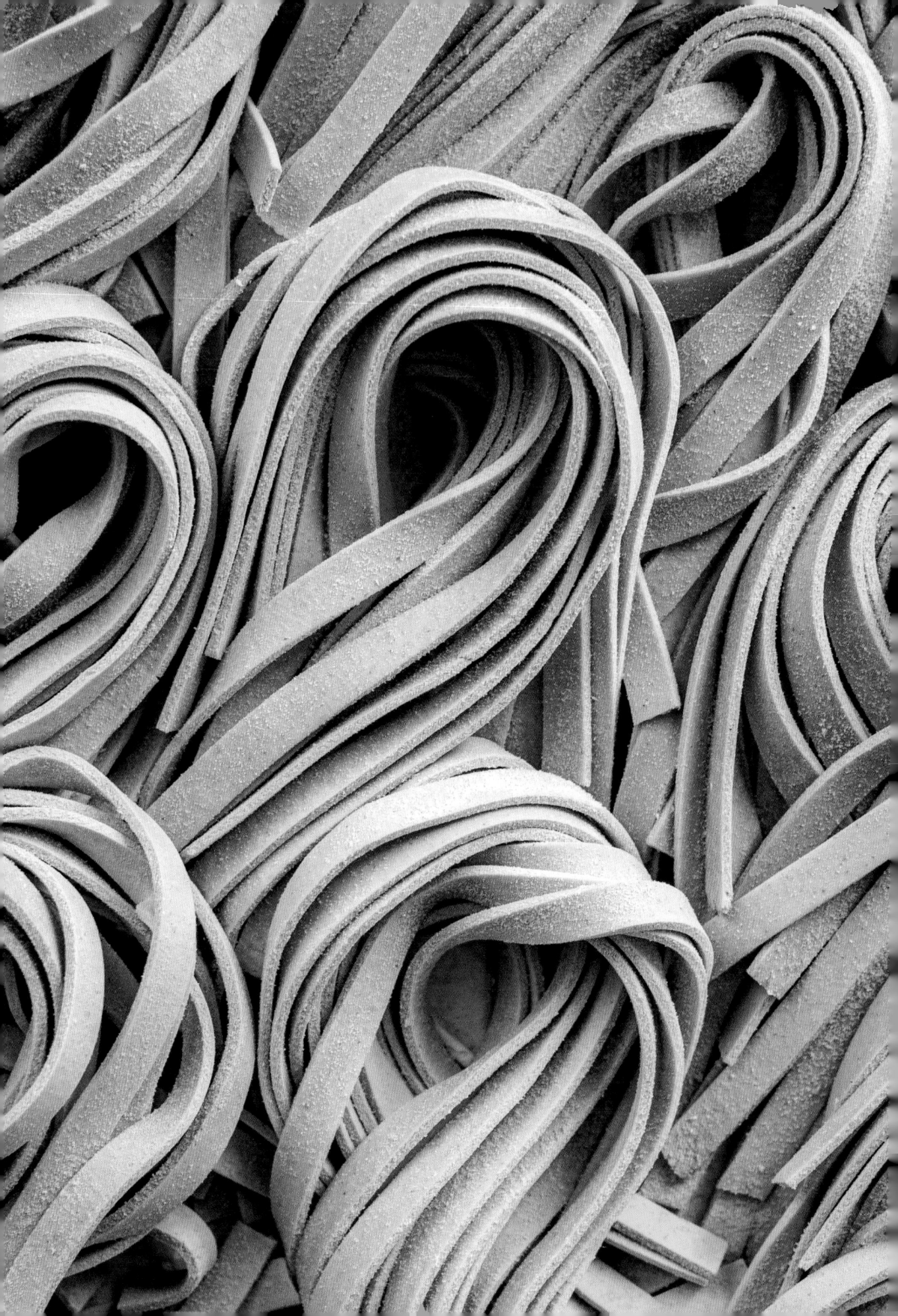

RAVIOLI DELLA NONNA IGEA RICOTTA AND SPINACH RAVIOLI

Nonna's ricotta and spinach ravioli are like memories folded into thin sheets of golden dough. When she's in her 'pasta zone,' there's no stopping her. Each raviolo is a masterpiece, crafted with care, focus and that signature Nonna Igea pride. Vincenzo recalls these being a fixture at every family gathering, and after two decades in the family, I feel the same. The filling is a luscious mix of creamy ricotta, vibrant spinach and a whisper of nutmeg – Nonna's secret touch that sets these apart. Watching her enjoy them is just as special: a precise slice down the centre, a forkful of sugo scooped up with finesse – it's a performance as much as a meal.

Nonna is generous with her knowledge, always reminding us, '*Più li fai e più brava diventi.* (The more you make them, the better you'll be.)' Her advice isn't about perfection; it's about showing up, making memories and passing down traditions. With this recipe, you'll bring a little piece of our family's legacy into your own kitchen.

SERVES 10 (PLUS LEFTOVERS TO FREEZE)
10 serves fresh egg pasta dough (see recipe, page 80), covered to prevent drying out
Tomato and basil sugo (see recipe, page 60) and Parmigiano Reggiano, to serve

RICOTTA AND SPINACH FILLING
350g (12.3 oz) fresh spinach
rock salt
600g (21.2 oz) strained ricotta
pinch of nutmeg
1 egg
150g (5.3 oz) Parmigiano Reggiano or Pecorino Romano, grated, plus extra depending on preference and taste

SPECIAL EQUIPMENT
rolling pin or pasta machine
ravioli or pastry cutter, or a sharp knife

1 To make the ricotta and spinach filling, remove the stalks from the spinach leaves and discard, then thoroughly wash the leaves. Strain then add to a medium pot. Add water to the pot and leave to boil on a low to medium heat.

2 Add a pinch of rock salt, mix it through and place the lid on, stirring occasionally so the leaves cook through. Once cooked, strain them by pressing the water out using a wooden spoon. Transfer to a plate, spread them out and leave to cool, straining again to remove excess water.

3 Once strained well, put the ricotta in a mixing bowl and break it down using a fork, then sprinkle in the nutmeg. Add an egg, beat, and mix it through well, before adding the Parmigiano.

4 Mix again with the fork then taste and add more Parmigiano for flavour, if you like.

5 Once the spinach has cooled, squeeze out any remaining water from the spinach, before chopping it up with a pair of scissors or knife. Add it to the ricotta and mix well with the fork. Add a generous amount of grated Parmigiano depending on preference and taste, and mix again. Once done, cover and set aside.

6 To make the ravioli, attach your pasta machine to the bench you are working on, and sprinkle some flour on it. Turn the nozzle to the widest setting. Cut a small portion of dough in preparation for the first sheet of pasta and press down on it slightly with the tips of your fingers before taking it through the pasta machine to flatten it.

7 Pass the dough through this first setting a few times, folding the sheet in half each time before feeding it back into the machine until you achieve a soft, smooth pasta sheet.

8 Set the machine to a thinner setting, typically one or two settings above the finest option (as settings vary by machine). Roll the pasta through 1–2 times, making sure the pasta sheet is long but not too thin, as it might tear when you cook the ravioli.

9 Lay the pasta sheet out on the board, and using a tablespoon and fork, add small portions of ravioli filling closer to one side of the sheet, about 2 finger-widths apart, being careful not to add too much!

10 Fold over the top section of the dough onto the bottom – be gentle and press down using the tips of your fingers so you bind the borders of the ravioli together.

RAVIOLI DELLA NONNA IGEA
RICOTTA & SPINACH RAVIOLI (CONT'D)

11 Using a pastry cutter or sharp knife, create half-moon ravioli pasta shapes, leaving a border around the filling so there is enough pasta to cook around each one, otherwise they will break open when cooking.

12 Using the edges of a fork, press down on the lip of each ravioli and create lines, so that each ravioli is tightly sealed. Repeat until you have made enough ravioli for your meal, or until you finish the dough.

13 Dust some flour on a tray and add each freshly made raviolo on it to rest before cooking them.

14 Cook the ravioli in an extra-large pot full of boiling water for at least 15 minutes or until the pasta is tender but not completely soft. As it is fresh pasta, the cooking time will depend on the thickness of the dough (which will differ for everyone, but Nonna keeps hers quite thick so the filling doesn't come out), so make sure to taste test while cooking and get the timing just right – keeping the ravioli al dente of course!

15 To serve, line a pot or extra-large serving bowl with Tomato and basil sugo, add a layer of cooked, strained ravioli, then another layer of sauce and grated Parmigiano, then another large serving of ravioli, and repeat the sauce and cheese until you have a bowl ready to serve up.

NONNA IGEA'S TIPS
- If you don't want to make a large batch of ravioli with the dough, you can combine it again to make another type of fresh pasta using your pasta machine or a knife. You can also use any extra long sheets to make lasagna.
- Leftover uncooked ravioli can be stored in an airtight container in the freezer for up to 6 months.

SPAGHETTI ALLA CHITARRA DELLA NONNA IGEA
THICK SQUARE SPAGHETTI

In Abruzzo, *spaghetti alla chitarra* – or *maccheroni alla chitarra* – is a pasta like no other, and made with a wooden tool that's as old-school as it gets: the chitarra. Named after a guitar because of its string-like wires, this ancient implement transforms pasta dough into beautifully thick rectangular strands. Watching Nonna use her chitarra is pure magic. She rolls the dough through those wires with such strength and grace, it looks effortless. When we try, however, it's more of a workout and far from graceful!

Every time we're back in Italy, Nonna makes batch after batch of this pasta just for us. She insists all pasta is created equal, but we're convinced this is her favourite. She just won't admit it!

This pasta's shape makes it a sauce magnet, perfect for Chitarra alla Teramana (see recipe, pages 129–30). It will transform your typical spaghetti and meatballs dish and you will be thanking Nonna all the way from your own kitchens. Another winning combination is Spaghetti allo scoglio (see recipe, page 104), with fresh seafood dancing between the strands.

SERVES 4–6

4 serves fresh egg pasta dough (see recipe, page 80), covered to prevent drying out, rested 30 minutes to 1 hour
plain (all purpose) or tipo '00' flour, for dusting

SPECIAL EQUIPMENT
pasta machine
chitarra (optional, if you can get your hands on one)
rolling pin

METHOD

1 Sprinkle some flour over the top of the pasta machine where you are about to feed the pasta through. Then cut a couple of slices – approximately 2–2.5cm (1 inch) thick, and feed them through the largest slot. Pass each one through the largest setting 3-4 times, folding it over in between each time.

2 Then work your way down to the thinner settings, only passing it through once at a time, until you get a smooth consistency but stop before the sheets are too thin. Each pasta machine is different, but you will typically need to stop 2–3 settings before the thinnest one. Always sprinkle added flour on top of the sheet before passing it through each option, to prevent it from sticking.

3 For the final step, if you do not have a chitarra, pass the pasta sheets through the correct option for spaghetti. By using the thicker sheets, you will get the desired shape. Don't be fooled, persist until you get thick strands.

IF YOU HAVE A CHITARRA

1 Sprinkle a generous amount of semolina or flour on your rolled pasta sheet to prevent the pasta from sticking to the strings. Then, lay the sheet of your rolled pasta over the chitarra strings.

2 Using a rolling pin, gently but firmly roll it over the sheet, in small bursts, not all the way forward and back at once, until the strings start to cut the pasta into perfect strands. Carefully lift the chitarra, and collect the cut pasta from beneath and repeat with the remaining sheets.

NONNA IGEA'S TIPS
- Keep some extra flour close by and sprinkle it over your hands as you knead the dough to get rid of the excess sticky bits that are likely to be all over them!
- Cover the remaining fresh pasta dough each time you finish using it to stop it from drying out and also so it doesn't continue to rise, especially if it's a warmer temperature in your kitchen.

GNOCCHI DI RICOTTA RICOTTA GNOCCHI

Vincenzo's speciality are what I call 'cheat's gnocchi' – divine pasta pillows made with ricotta instead of potatoes. They're quick to roll out and a bit more beginner-friendly than traditional gnocchi, mainly because there are fewer variables! Vincenzo has taught this recipe in his cooking classes, and everyone is always amazed by how well they turn out. Made with ricotta, flour, an egg and a hint of Pecorino, these gnocchi don't compromise on flavour.

When Vincenzo created this recipe, we couldn't believe how beautifully they turned out. More oval than our traditional gnocchi and slightly al dente in texture, they're delicious with sugo, pesto or just brown butter and sage.

SERVES 4–6

- 500g (17.6 oz) ricotta (use the dry variety or strain overnight in the fridge to release excess liquid)
- 1 egg
- 300g (10.6 oz) plain (all purpose) or tipo '00' flour, plus extra for dusting
- 3–4 tbsp (2 oz) finely grated Pecorino Romano
- 1 tbsp rock salt

SPECIAL EQUIPMENT
rolling pin

METHOD

1 Add the ricotta to a bowl and press down on it using a fork, then crack an egg into it. Beat well and mix through. Add a sprinkle of flour and start to combine, before also adding the Pecorino and mixing it through. Pour in a small portion of flour at a time, combining it before adding more. Once you have mixed in all of the flour, transfer the dough onto a wooden board and start to gently knead it until the dough softens and is not sticky. Create a ball and leave it to the side, covered with a large bowl placed upside down, for 3–5 minutes.

2 Dust a surface where you will prepare your gnocchi with some flour and put the dough on top. Using a rolling pin, roll gently forward and back until you flatten the dough to around 2.5cm (1 inch) thickness. Cut into horizontal strips and then roll each one into round, snake-like shapes before using a pastry cutter, dough scraper or sharp knife to cut the lengths into small pillows.

3 Place the gnocchi on a floured tray to prevent sticking and if you don't intend to cook them immediately, freeze them on the tray, then transfer to a sealed bag once frozen. If cooking the same day, don't leave the gnocchi out for too long to avoid a gummy texture.

4 To cook them, bring a large pot of water to a boil, adding the rock salt to dissolve. Gently add the fresh gnocchi, stirring occasionally with a wooden spoon to prevent sticking. Cover and cook them until the gnocchi rise to the surface. If you're unsure, taste one (or two!) to test their texture. Strain well using a hand sieve and toss gently with your favourite sauce to combine. Each portion is 1 handful per person – they're much lighter than their potato cousins, so you'll likely devour more!

VINCENZO'S TIPS

- You might be able to convince your children to help roll these out – it's like edible play-dough. Our eldest son Sebastian loves seeing the result of the 'snakes' he rolls out!
- Cutting the gnocchi into similar sizes helps them cook in the same length of time.
- Avoid semolina flour, as it makes the pasta harder and drier. This recipe needs a softer dough since the ricotta already makes it denser than traditional gnocchi.
- When combining ricotta gnocchi with the sauce, use a wooden spoon to gently mix together, as the gnocchi can break easily. Avoid using a spoon or fork.
- Use frozen gnocchi within 6 months. You can cook them from frozen – there's no need to thaw them out.

GNOCCHI DELLA NONNA IGEA POTATO GNOCCHI

These gnocchi leave me speechless every time. Soft, delicate and melt-in-your-mouth good, they are the ultimate version of perfect pillows and I can't be convinced otherwise. I'll happily eat three bowls and call it a feast. On our last trip to Italy, even our four-year-old son, Sebastian, showed he's a natural, gleefully polishing off several plates. We love serving them with Tomato and basil sugo (see recipe, page 60) or Pesto al basilico (see recipe, page 64).

Hailing from Abruzzo's Teramo province, Nonna Igea's gnocchi are also known as *li surgitt* and they're not what you might be used to. No fork indents, no chewiness – just pillowy perfection. Watching Nonna make them is witnessing a maestra at work. She effortlessly crafts up to 10kg (22 lb) in one go, her hands moving with a rhythm only decades of experience can bring.

After 17 years of learning from Nonna, I feel as if I have finally started to master this cherished recipe. Vincenzo says, 'Food brings people together,' and I dream of sitting one day at my own table as a nonna, watching my family devour these gnocchi and knowing I've kept her legacy alive.

SERVES 10
5–6 potatoes (Nonna prefers yellow potatoes or Yukon Gold), peeled, washed and cut into small chunks
1 egg
300g (10.6 oz) plain (all purpose) or tipo '00' flour, plus extra for kneading
1 tbsp rock salt

SPECIAL EQUIPMENT
potato ricer (or you can use a fork)

METHOD

1 Fill a pot with water and bring to a boil. Add the potato, cover and cook for about 10 minutes, or until a fork easily slides through. Don't overcook or you'll ruin the texture.

2 Press small batches of potato through the ricer onto onto a clean surface or chopping board, then spread to cool. Once slightly cooled, gather the potato into a mound, create a well, and crack in the egg. Beat by hand and mix through the potato.

3 Gradually add flour, combining until the mixture forms a dough. It may be crumbly at first, but keep working it until smooth, adding the flour as you go and scraping any from your surface and sticking it back into the dough. Test the dough by cutting a piece and touching the inside – it should be soft and only slightly sticky. Shape into a loaf.

4 Cut the dough into small portions and roll them into long 'snakes' using both hands working your way outward from the centre of each one. Next, cut these into small diamond-shaped pillows by cutting the lengths on a bias (diagonally).

5 Place the gnocchi on a floured tray to prevent sticking and if you don't intend to cook them immediately, freeze them on the tray, then transfer to a sealed bag once frozen. If cooking the same day, don't leave gnocchi out for too long, to avoid a gummy texture.

6 To cook them, bring a large pot of water to a boil, adding the rock salt to dissolve. Gently add the fresh gnocchi, stirring occasionally with a wooden spoon to prevent sticking. Cover and cook them for about 3 minutes or until the gnocchi rise to the surface. If you're unsure, taste one and adjust the cooking time. Strain well using a hand sieve and toss with your favourite sauce to combine.

NONNA IGEA'S TIPS
- If the riced potatoes are too hot, or have cooled completely, the gnocchi won't turn out right.
- If the gnocchi are too sticky, add a dusting of flour. Once the dough binds, stop! Overworking or adding too much flour will make them hard instead of pillowy.
- Only add gnocchi to water once it is boiling or they'll absorb too much water and lose their texture. Once it does boil, add the gnocchi and strain as they rise to the surface. Don't wait for all of them to come up – this is a gradual process.

PRIMI
(BUT MOSTLY PASTA)

PRIMI (BUT MOSTLY PASTA)

Here we dive into a tribute to the primi, the first course of a traditional Italian meal and a showcase of the dishes that define our cuisine. These creations bring comfort, celebration and connection to the table, with pasta as their undisputed star. But while it's a pasta party, the primi category is broad, so we've also included a few exceptions like creamy mushroom risotto and the irresistibly delicious sausage polenta.

Our collection of recipes honours dishes that have stood the test of time, including authentic versions of classics loved around the world, from a perfectly spicy Penne all'arrabbiata to the delicate flavours of Gnocchi alla Sorrentina. We've combined these with another serving of family favourites passed down from our matriarch, Nonna Igea. Master them and you might just earn your own honorary Nonna title. Fair warning: this title comes with strong opinions.

With the seemingly endless variety of pasta shapes, the possibilities are infinite, but let's be real: there are some dishes we simply can't live without. Life's too short for bad Pasta al pomodoro or bland Cacio e pepe, and as Vincenzo says, 'An Italian without pasta is like an opera without music – it just doesn't exist.'

Think of this section as your pasta bible – a guide to everything from the perfect Aglio, olio e peperoncino to Nonna's legendary Timballo, which is her delicate, crepe-layered lasagna worth every minute of preparation. You'll also find Vincenzo's tried-and-true signature dishes, like his no-cream Carbonara and silky-smooth Linguine alle vongole, both of which are his all-time favourite dishes.

In our home, pasta is often the answer. It brings comfort when our young boys are sad, adds joy to a special occasion, and is the perfect dish when guests arrive – planned or last-minute. A plate of pasta is filled with happiness, and hopefully this feeling transcends from our kitchen into yours too.

BUCATINI ALL'AMATRICIANA

This dish is sometimes described as a carbonara with red sugo. It originated years ago in the small town of Amatrice and has been made even more famous in Rome. The signature sugo relies on three key factors: the crispiness of the guanciale, the richness of the San Marzano tomatoes and a generous dusting of Pecorino Romano. This combination makes the dish salty, savoury and spicy all at once. Like most Italian dishes, we rely on sourcing the right ingredients. Find them yourself and you will have zero regrets when you serve this up.

SERVES 2–3
200g (7 oz) guanciale
800g (28.2 oz) canned whole peeled Italian tomatoes
1 tbsp rock salt, plus a pinch for seasoning
black pepper
Pecorino Romano, finely grated, qb
300g (10.6 oz) bucatini pasta
dried chilli flakes (optional)

SPECIAL EQUIPMENT
immersion blender

METHOD

1 Slice the skin off the guanciale using a sharp knife, and discard it. Cut the guanciale into thin slices, then strips, so each piece has fat on the outside and meat in the middle.

2 In a bowl, gently crush the tomatoes using an immersion blender until it becomes a smooth sauce.

3 Heat a large frying pan over medium–low heat. Once it starts to warm, add the guanciale strips and sauté for about 5 minutes, or until they turn crispy and the oil is released from the fat. Add the tomato, mix it through, then increase the heat to medium and add a pinch of rock salt to season. Let the sauce cook for 20 minutes, stirring occasionally and lowering the heat if it starts to bubble. Just before the sauce finishes cooking, add a generous amount of pepper, before mixing through some grated Pecorino.

4 While the sauce is cooking, bring a large pot of water to a rolling boil, add rock salt, allow to dissolve and then cook your pasta according to the packet instructions. Once al dente, reserve ½ mug pasta water.

5 Using tongs, transfer the pasta to the pan with the sauce and mix everything together. Toss well and add a splash of reserved pasta water to help thicken the sauce, then toss again. Add more Pecorino (always) and toss one last time.

6 Plate the pasta and top with guanciale from the pan. To serve, sprinkle more grated Pecorino and pepper on top of each portion, and even some dried chilli for added spice.

VINCENZO'S TIPS

- If you struggle to find good quality guanciale, you can substitute with pancetta. If you use bacon, maybe it's best you just don't tell me.
- If the guanciale does not have good-quality fat, it might not create enough oil in the pan, so just add a touch of EVOO to help make up for this.
- Be mindful of the salt content. Guanciale is already quite salty, so adjust how much salt you add accordingly to ensure the dish is not overly seasoned.
- To check if your sauce is ready, scrape a line across the pan with a wooden spoon. If the sauce slowly comes back together, it's perfect. If it stays runny, keep cooking!
- For extra crunch, set aside a portion of the crispy guanciale on paper towel before adding the tomatoes to the pan and use it as a garnish. I like leaving it in the sauce – it keeps adding flavour as it cooks, making the sauce irresistible!

SPAGHETTI ALLA CARBONARA

Do Italians a favour and stop messing with traditional recipes. Carbonara is sacred – no cream, no cream cheese and definitely no peas. This iconic Roman dish is loved worldwide, yet is so often ruined by unnecessary changes. Cream has no place here. True carbonara is beautifully simple: just eggs, Pecorino, pepper, pasta water, guanciale and pasta – nothing more, nothing less.

When Vincenzo filmed himself reacting to a famous chef making a disastrous carbonara, followed by one of himself making an authentic version (without cream!), his carbonara revolution began. His version even earned him the approval of the Romans themselves. Now, people everywhere are ditching fake versions, realising that authentic Italian dishes aren't complicated and don't need altering.

SERVES 2–3 (OR IF YOU'RE VINCENZO, JUST 1!)
200g (7 oz) guanciale, skin removed, fat left on
300g (10.6 oz) spaghetti pasta (see tips)
½ tbsp rock salt
4 eggs (1 egg yolk for every 100g pasta, plus 1 whole egg for the pan)
freshly cracked black pepper
90g (3.2 oz) Pecorino Romano, finely grated

METHOD

1 Slice the guanciale into large strips, then smaller strips so there is fat on one side and meat in the middle.

2 In a large frying pan over medium–low heat, add the guanciale. To avoid burning, move it around using a wooden spoon. Cook for a few minutes, or until golden brown and crispy, but still tender. Remove from the heat and transfer to a plate lined with paper towel to rest. Save the guanciale fat in the pan to cook with later.

3 Bring a large pot of water to a rolling boil, add rock salt, allow to dissolve and then cook your pasta according to the packet instructions.

4 Separate 3 egg yolks from their whites and place them in a small bowl. Crack a whole egg into the same bowl.

Beat using a fork until combined. Add a generous amount of pepper and mix again. Gradually add some Pecorino. Mix and continue to add Pecorino until you reach a thick, creamy consistency.

5 Once the pasta is ready, place the pan with guanciale oil over medium–low heat. Using tongs, transfer the pasta to the pan, allowing some pasta water to drop in. Mix, then scoop up a mug of pasta water and add some to the pan. Mix through.

6 With the pasta water pan on the cooktop (heat off), rest the frying pan on top. The steam from the pasta water will help continue to cook the pasta.

7 Add a touch more pasta water, a handful of guanciale and the egg mixture. Mix using a wooden spoon. Continue to add pasta water slowly, then toss well to combine the pasta and egg mixture until it thickens. There is no time to wait – as this dish sits, the sauce can start to dry out and the pasta will stick together. Fresh off the stove, it's heavenly. Wait too long and it's just not the same. Serve onto plates, topping with leftover sauce and a few strips of remaining guanciale. Garnish with a generous amount of pepper – it's essential!

VINCENZO'S TIPS
- Sourcing guanciale can be hard. A fantastic alternative is pancetta, and it's more readily available at butchers and delis. While you don't need to use EVOO for the guanciale (as it releases its own oil), you may need a tablespoon or two for pancetta.
- This dish is particularly good with spaghetti alla chitarra (also known as spaghetti quadrati, see recipe, page 91). If you can't find or make that, you could use thick spaghetti such as spaghetti no.7 or spaghettoni, or use rigatoni instead.
- If you're increasing the serves, follow this cheese-to-pasta ratio: for every 100g of pasta use at least 30g of grated Pecorino. (You can never go wrong with adding extra, just never less!)
- If your carbonara isn't served right away and starts to feel a bit stiff, add extra pasta water and warm it on a low heat. A little splash will prevent the sauce from becoming too thick and keep it creamy.

SPAGHETTI ALLO SCOGLIO PASTA WITH SEAFOOD

This recipe is our family's take on a coastal classic, *pasta allo scoglio*, a specialty of Vincenzo's papà, Paolo. It's the kind of dish that every seafood restaurant along the Italian coast vies to perfect, but in our opinion, Paolo's version reigns supreme.

This dish is a delightful combination of the freshest seafood, a splash of white wine, and the unexpected creaminess that comes from the pasta water. As you cook it at home, the aromas will transport you straight to Vincenzo's hometown of Pescara. Unlike many seafood pastas with a heavy tomato sauce, this dish celebrates the pure, fresh flavours of the sea.

SERVES 4

extra virgin olive oil (EVOO), qb
1–2 garlic cloves
2–3 calamari or squid
½ glass white wine, preferably dry
300g (10.6 oz) cherry tomatoes, halved
12 prawns or scampi, shells intact
1kg (35.3 oz) mussels, cleaned (see tip, page 206)
500g (17.6 oz) vongole (clams), cleaned (see recipe, page 206)
rock salt
small bunch of flat-leaf (Italian) parsley leaves, chopped
500g (17.6 oz) spaghetti, linguine or chitarra pasta
black pepper, qb

METHOD

1 Place a large frying pan over medium heat and add a generous drizzle of EVOO. Add the garlic, and stir it around using a wooden spoon to infuse the oil, then add the calamari or squid, mixing it again while it simmers.

2 Pour in the white wine and add the tomato. Cook for up to 6 minutes, or until the tomato softens and starts to break down. Add the prawns or scampi and combine for 2 minutes, before also adding the mussels and vongole. Mix in a pinch of salt and a large pinch of parsley, then stir to combine. Leave to cook for 3–5 minutes, or until all the shells open (some will remain closed and will need to be discarded). Remove from heat.

3 Bring a large pot of water to a rolling boil, add rock salt, allow to dissolve and then cook your pasta according to the packet instructions. Once al dente, reserve ½ mug pasta water then, using tongs, add the pasta to the pan of seafood. Place over medium–low heat. Add about half of the pasta water and use the tongs or a wooden spoon to combine. Lower the heat and let it gently simmer while the pasta water helps to combine the ingredients and thicken the sauce.

4 Toss well so all ingredients are smothering the pasta, before serving. Portion onto plates and garnish with remaining parsley and pepper.

PAPÀ PAOLO'S TIPS

- Avoid using a sweet wine if possible, to ensure it doesn't overpower the dish.
- The cooking time for the cherry tomatoes will depend on how fresh they are. The more tender, the less time they need.
- For both mussels and vongole, discard any with damaged or broken shells, or that are open, before you cook them.
- Don't overcook the seafood as it will dry out and lose the intensity of its flavour. If you're worried, turn the heat down and cook more gently.
- Don't try to pry open any mussels and vongole that remain shut once cooked.
- It's a MUST to use a long pasta so you can twirl the seafood between the strands.

CACIO E PEPE

If there was ever a dish that should be named after Vincenzo, it's this one. His love affair with Pecorino is difficult to compete with (as his wife, I should know!), and since this recipe highlights his favourite cheese with just one other ingredient, black pepper, it would seem it was made for him.

Cacio e pepe is a Roman dish, translating to cheese and pepper, and it is the best version of a mac and cheese you will ever taste in your life. Don't even try to argue about it. It's one of four famous Roman pasta dishes with just a few ingredients, so you only need to learn some simple tricks to master it at home. The goal is to create a creamy, emulsified sauce that coats each strand of long, thick pasta with the most intense flavour of Pecorino and freshly ground black pepper. Take your time to get it right and you will not regret it.

SERVES 2
1 tbsp rock salt
freshly cracked black pepper
200g (7 oz) Spaghetti alla chitarra (see recipe, page 91) or store-bought spaghetto quadrato or spaghettoni pasta (just don't use anything thin as it won't soak up the sauce in the same way)
100g (3.5 oz) Pecorino Romano, finely grated

METHOD

1 Bring a large pot of water to a rolling boil, add rock salt, allow to dissolve, and then cook your pasta for 2–3 minutes less than the recommended cooking time on the packet. Trust in the process; if you overcook it, it won't absorb the sauce.

2 Meanwhile, place a separate large frying pan or sauté pan over low heat and cover the base of the pan with pepper – be generous. Toast for 2 minutes, then switch off the heat.

3 In a small bowl, combine the Pecorino and some more pepper.

4 Using tongs, transfer the pasta to the pan with the pepper. Scoop up a mug of pasta water and add it to the pasta and pepper. Add enough water to cover the pasta, but don't let it drown.

5 Cook the pasta for 2 minutes over medium heat while continuously stirring – don't hesitate, just stir! Scoop another mug of pasta water and put just a splash into the bowl of cheese and pepper, then mix really well with a fork. Gradually add more pasta water, mixing until the Pecorino cream becomes a thick paste.

6 Rest the pan on top of the large pot of pasta water (heat off) so the steam continues to cook the pasta.

7 Make sure there is some pasta water left in the pasta pan before adding the Pecorino cream. Toss well, adding a touch more pasta water as needed to keep it moving. Toss to melt the cheese. Using tongs, plate the pasta and top with extra Pecorino cream from the pan and a generous sprinkle of black pepper. Don't hold back. Eat it immediately, especially if you made it for one – right out of the pan!

VINCENZO'S TIPS
- This can only be made with Pecorino Romano, so once you source it, make this right away! It has a distinct flavour and makes the creamiest sauce.
- The Pecorino is best grated finely for this dish to work. Keep an eye on the ratio; for example, use 150g (5.3 oz) Pecorino with 300g (10.5 oz) pasta.
- The science behind this dish comes from using the starchy pasta water. Make sure you save it, as it is a key ingredient.
- Rushing this dish can lead to a watery sauce or clumps of cheese. Follow the steps carefully and ensure the pan isn't too hot when you add the pasta.

PASTA ALLA GRICIA

This Roman dish is the love child of Carbonara and Cacio e pepe. The silky texture of cheese combined with the crispness of the guanciale are an undeniable match – your tastebuds will thank you with every bite. Vincenzo first discovered this pasta at a typical local trattoria in Rome and couldn't believe it was his first time trying it! The owner boasted about it being one of the oldest pasta dishes in Roman history and Vincenzo made it his mission to recreate it in the most authentic way possible.

Don't go past this thick, creamy pasta sauce made of just two key ingredients: Pecorino and guanciale. It's almost never about adding more but, instead, about using ingredients wisely. This pasta is tossed in the rendered fat of the guanciale, smothered with melted cheese and finished off with a hint of black pepper. It's melt-in-your-mouth simplicity.

SERVES 2
150g (5.3 oz) guanciale
freshly cracked black pepper
1 tbsp rock salt
250g (8.8 oz) mezze maniche pasta (or any short pasta of your choice)
150g (5.3 oz) Pecorino Romano, finely grated, plus extra to serve

METHOD

1 Remove and discard the peppery side from the guanciale (and any skin), then cut it into thick pieces before slicing thinly.

2 Heat a large frying pan or sauté pan over medium heat, add a generous amount of pepper and toast for 1 minute. Add the guanciale and cook, stirring occasionally, for a few minutes, or until crispy and golden brown. If it starts to burn, lower the heat. Once ready, transfer the guanciale to paper towel to drain. Keep the rendered fat in the pan and turn off the heat.

3 Bring a large pot of water to a rolling boil, add rock salt, allow to dissolve and then cook your pasta according to the packet instructions.

4 While the pasta is cooking, combine the Pecorino and more pepper in a small bowl. Just before the pasta has finished cooking, scoop up a mug of pasta water, gradually adding some to the bowl, then mix until thick and creamy. You might not need all the water; don't allow it to become runny.

5 Once the pasta is ready, use a hand-held sieve to transfer the pasta to the pan with the guanciale fat, allowing some pasta water to drop in. Remove the pot with the pasta water from the heat, leaving the water inside.

6 Place the pan with the pasta over low heat. Stir in a splash of reserved pasta water. Toss well.

7 Rest the pan with the pasta on top of the large pot of pasta water (heat off). The steam from the pasta water will continue to cook the pasta. Pour the cheese mixture into the pasta pan. Stir until fully melted. Gradually add more pasta water to help melt the cheese and thicken the sauce, before tossing again. Add one last splash of pasta water, along with the guanciale (reserve some pieces for garnish) and toss again. Serve with more creamy cheese from the pan over the top, the reserved guanciale and pepper. Provide extra Pecorino on the side for those who want even more – no Pecorino, no party, right?

VINCENZO'S TIPS
- The dish has a really strong kick thanks to all the pepper we add. If you don't love a strong peppery kick, just use less. Let your tastebuds be your guide.
- My favourite pasta to use is mezze maniche, but it can be tricky to find. If you can't track any down, use any short shape, such as rigatoni or penne.
- This is not a recipe where you clean as you go! You need to keep not only the pan with the rendered guanciale fat for later use, but the pot filled with pasta water too.

LINGUINE ALLE VONGOLE PASTA WITH CLAMS

For Vincenzo, there is no better dish. Honestly, when we're in Italy, he eats it countless times. Now both our sons, Sebastian and Alessandro, love it too. I mean, how could they not, especially when they get to slurp each vongole out of its shell? Vincenzo and his papà, Paolo, compete and converse regularly on how to make it – and who makes it better – but the key ingredients remain the same, and often the flavour relies heavily on the vongole.

You'll need to start this recipe at least 4 hours before you plan on serving, to soak the vongole. When it is hard to source vongole like those in Italy, good substitutes are clams. Are they the same? No, but they will give you a delicious alternative. And if you know how to toss the pasta while it's in the pan, do it! This process, known as *mantecatura*, will create the creamy, full-bodied consistency and texture that make all the difference.

SERVES 3–4

- 1kg (35.3 oz) vongole (clams), shells scrubbed clean
- 1 tbsp sea salt
- 4–6 tbsp extra virgin olive oil (EVOO), plus extra for drizzling
- 2 garlic cloves
- bunch of flat-leaf (Italian) parsley, stems and leaves roughly chopped, plus extra to serve
- ½ glass white wine or prosecco
- 400g (10.6 oz) linguine pasta
- finely chopped fresh chilli or dried chilli flakes, to serve (optional)

METHOD

1 Place vongole to a bowl filled with cold water (enough to cover them) and 3 heaped tbsp sea salt. Leave to soak for 4 hours, changing the water after 2 hours, to remove the most amount of grit and impurities. Drain using a colander and leave to the side.

2 Bring a large pot of water to a rolling boil, add 1 tbsp sea salt and allow to dissolve.

3 While waiting for the water to boil, add the EVOO to a large frying pan over low heat. Grate the garlic directly into the pan. Add half the parsley and cook for 30 seconds, stirring gently with a wooden spoon. Add the vongole and mix until coated. Increase the heat to medium and add the wine or prosecco and 1 tsp sea salt. Cover with a lid or foil, leaving the steam to develop inside and cook the vongole.

4 While covered, the vongole will start to open. After 3 minutes, remove the lid and use the wooden spoon to mix again and check how many still need to open. Cover again and cook for 2 more minutes, or until you no longer hear them opening. If there are just a couple still unopened, they may stay this way. Don't leave to cook too much longer as once overcooked vongole become chewy and tough to eat. Remove from heat.

5 Once the water is at a rolling boil, add the pasta and cook 2–3 minutes less than in the packet instructions.

6 Reserve ½ mug pasta water then drain the pasta. Add the pasta and half the reserved pasta water to the vongole pan and stir through. This helps the pasta continue cooking while also creating a creamier consistency. Keep mixing gently and tossing and cook for up to 2 minutes, adding a generous sprinkle of remaining parsley as you go. If it dries up at any stage, add another portion of pasta water, tossing it really well, making sure the heat is on medium-low.

7 Serve hot with another sprinkle of parsley, pepper and some fresh or dried chilli, if you like. For added richness, drizzle some EVOO over the top and enjoy the taste of the Mediterranean in every bite.

VINCENZO'S TIPS

- Try to source the highest quality vongole you can get your hands on from your local fishmonger. Some supermarkets stock frozen ones, which are fine to use too.
- If you prefer no alcohol, chop up a large handful of fresh cherry tomatoes and add them to the pan instead, letting them soften completely and release their juices. This will strengthen the flavour.

CONCHIGLIONI RIPIENI AL FORNO STUFFED PASTA SHELLS

This dish is all about the salty mixture of ricotta and spinach filling, made even more flavoursome thanks to Nonna Igea's secret spice weapon, which adds a subtle, nutty aroma: nutmeg. With classic tomato sugo smothering the pasta and melted mozzarella stuffed into every crevice, every part of this oven-bake is filled with flavour. While it may look intensive to prepare, the whole process from start to finish takes no longer than 30 minutes – yet it will likely be devoured in three!

Want to take it a step further? Use fresh buffalo mozzarella to finish this off. No stringy packet mozzarella in this house, ever. So remove it from yours and enjoy the difference. We are not dramatic, we are Italian. Get rid of the fake stuff in your kitchens and feel an overwhelming sense of pride with every bite.

SERVES 4

- 2–3 tbsp extra virgin olive oil (EVOO)
- 2 garlic cloves, crushed
- 700g (24.7 oz) bottle store-bought passata or use homemade (see recipe, page 74)
- salt and pepper
- small bunch of basil, whole or torn
- 300g (10.6 oz) conchiglioni pasta (large pasta shells)
- 1 tbsp rock salt
- Pecorino Romano, for sprinkling
- 1 fresh fior di latte or buffalo mozzarella ball

SPINACH AND RICOTTA FILLING

- 300g (10.6 oz) baby spinach (fresh or frozen)
- 400g (14.1 oz) ricotta
- 3 tbsp finely grated Pecorino Romano
- sprinkle of nutmeg (freshly grated or ground)
- salt and pepper
- 1 egg

METHOD

1 To make the sauce, heat the EVOO in a medium saucepan over medium–low heat. Cook the garlic, stirring occasionally, for about 2 minutes, or until fragrant and golden. Stir in the passata, then season with salt and pepper. Mix in the basil leaves, reserving a few, and simmer for 20 minutes, stirring occasionally.

2 Meanwhile, bring a large pot of water to a rolling boil, add rock salt, and allow to dissolve. Add the pasta and cook for 2 minutes less than in the packet instructions. Drain and let the shells cool for a few minutes until they can be handled.

3 To prepare the filling, cook the spinach in a frying pan over medium heat, stirring occasionally, until wilted. Add a little water if needed to prevent sticking. Drain any excess water, then mix the spinach (once cooled) and ricotta in a bowl until smooth. Stir in the Pecorino, nutmeg, salt and pepper. Beat the egg, then add it to the spinach mixture. Use a fork to combine thoroughly.

4 Preheat the oven to 180°C (360°F) and generously cover the base of a baking dish with some of the sauce.

5 To assemble the stuffed pasta shells, use a tablespoon to fill the open part of each shell with the spinach and ricotta filling. Arrange the shells in the dish starting from the outside edge and working towards the centre. Top with more sauce, sprinkle with Pecorino and pieces of mozzarella, breaking the mozzarella into small chunks with your hands. Bake for 20 minutes.

6 Remove from the oven and let rest for 10 minutes, then serve warm to enjoy the melted cheese and creamy ricotta filling. Scoop up the shells whole, garnish with the reserved basil, and offer extra sugo on the side.

VINCENZO'S TIPS
- The amount of pasta in the ingredients is just a guide. You may want to add more depending on the serves you need or to fill a larger baking dish.
- If you don't like spinach, don't use it! Shells filled with ricotta and (extra) nutmeg are equally delicious. You could also include a hint of lemon zest for added freshness.
- Be generous when adding the sugo to your baking dish, so that the shells stay moist while cooking.

LE SCRIPPELLE NONNA IGEA'S CREPES

Nonna's crepes are legendary – thin, soft and airy. Once you master them – you need just a few ingredients and a touch of precision – you'll likely find yourself making batch after batch! It may surprise you how versatile these crepes can be. They feature in some of Nonna's most beloved recipes, like Timballo alla Teramana (see recipe, page 122) and Ricotta and spinach cannelloni (see recipe, page 117). You can even make them into dessert by drizzling honey or melted chocolate on top. They never fail, even using her signature 'Nonna measurements', so don't be deterred.

The first time I watched Nonna make crepes, her speed and skill amazed me. She juggled three pans, flipped crepes with ease and moved with graceful precision. When it was my turn, she wisely told me to start with one pan, assuring me that 'experience brings skill'. She was right! Now, I use two pans – and as long as no one's watching, I manage pretty well.

MAKES 12 CREPES
4 large eggs
salt
4 tbsp plain (all-purpose) flour, sifted
extra virgin olive oil (EVOO) or unsalted butter, for greasing

METHOD

1 Crack 1 egg carefully from the top so that just a small part of the eggshell breaks. Pour the egg into a bowl and put the larger piece of the shell to the side. This is the measuring cup for your crepes (and one of my favourite Nonna hacks). Crack the other eggs as you normally would, adding them to the bowl and discarding the remaining shells. Whisk the eggs swiftly for 5 minutes, or until small bubbles form on top.

2 Wash the reserved eggshell well. Fill it with water and add this to the whisked egg. Repeat twice more, then mix your eggs once again. Add a generous pinch of salt and mix for another 3 minutes. Add half the flour and mix through, then add more as you go. The texture needs to be smooth and dense, not runny. The amount of flour you need will be based on the size of the egg. Add a touch more flour if it appears too runny, or more water if it is too thick.

3 Place a small or medium frying pan over medium heat and use a paper towel soaked in EVOO to coat the pan, or add some butter and melt.

4 Pick up the pan by the handle and, with your other hand, half fill a ladle with batter and pour it into the pan, moving the pan around on an angle as you pour. This will help it spread thinly over the base of the pan. Place the pan back on the heat, wait 10–15 seconds, then use a fork to lift the outer edge of the crepe to check whether it has begun to cook through. If it has, peel back one corner of the crepe, keep peeling, then quickly flip over (you can also use a turner, just be delicate). Cook on the other side for 15–20 seconds, or until the crepe is cooked through. Repeat with remaining batter, greasing the pan between each crepe.

NONNA IGEA'S TIPS
- Try not to overthink the measurements for this one! I have used the egg as the measuring cup for this recipe every time I make this, and the crepes turn out perfectly.
- If you need to make a different number of crepes, keep in mind that for every 3 crepes you will need 1 egg and 1 tbsp flour.
- A non-stick skillet or traditional crepe pan is ideal. The surface should be lightly greased and heated enough so the batter sizzles slightly when poured.
- Preheat the pan to medium heat, then reduce to medium–low when cooking. This prevents the crepes from burning or browning too quickly.
- Don't pour batter into the middle of the pan – it will make the crepe too thick
- Don't add too much batter to the pan. Take your time, and if you get a hole in one, finish making it, then add a little more batter to the next one. What you want to avoid is making them too thick.

CANNELLONI RICOTTA E SPINACI DELLA NONNA IGEA

Once you taste cannelloni made with homemade crepes instead of pasta sheets, it's hard to go back. These crepes, or *scrippelle*, are lighter than traditional pasta dough, quick to make and hail from Nonna Igea's province of Teramo in Abruzzo. Trust Nonna – she knows best.

Nonna's cannelloni are filled with ricotta and spinach, topped with tomato and basil sauce, then baked until the mozzarella melts perfectly and the edges crisp slightly. Bake a tray to enjoy now and freeze another batch for later – once you learn how to make the crepes, this dish is a breeze.

This recipe holds special memories for us. It was one of the first dishes we prepared for family and friends in Australia when we catered our engagement party. Naturally, we underestimated and didn't make enough. Lesson learned: think like a nonna and always be overprepared!

SERVES 4–6
12 freshly made crepes (see recipe, page 114)
1 batch Tomato and basil sugo, cooled (see recipe, page 60)
Parmigiano Reggiano, for sprinkling
50g butter, cut to small cubes

CANNELLONI FILLING
500g (17.6 oz) baby spinach (fresh or frozen)
400g (14.1 oz) ricotta
3 tbsp Parmigiano Reggiano
sprinkle of nutmeg (freshly grated or ground)
pinch of salt
1 egg

METHOD

1 To prepare the cannelloni filling, cook the spinach in a frying pan over medium heat, stirring occasionally, until wilted. Add a little water if needed to prevent sticking. Drain the spinach using a sieve, pressing down hard with a fork to allow any excess to drip out. Set aside to cool.

2 Place the ricotta in a bowl and break it down with a fork, then mix through the cooled spinach until well combined. Add the Parmigiano, nutmeg and salt, then mix again. Crack an egg into the mixture and beat well with the fork until it disappears and binds the ingredients together.

3 Preheat the oven to 200°C (392°F).

4 To assemble the cannelloni, place 1 crepe on a flat surface, then spread a small portion of the sauce all over, and sprinkle Parmigiano on top. Add a spoonful of the filling to one edge of the crepe and press down slightly using the back of the spoon so it spreads lengthways but not right up to the edges. Begin rolling up the crepe carefully, then fold in the edges before continuing to roll it closed. Repeat until all the crepes are filled.

5 Use a cube of butter to grease a baking dish, then spread a scoop of the remaining sauce over the base of the dish. Arrange the cannelloni in the dish and gently spread more sauce over the top using a tablespoon. Don't drown them or they will end up soggy, but don't skip this step or they will end up dry – and Nonna will not be impressed!

6 Scatter the remaining cubes of butter on top of and in between some of the cannelloni. This will help them stay moist and cook through. Sprinkle over some Parmigiano, then bake for 15–20 minutes, or place in your fridge to cook the next day. Once the cannelloni have finished baking, remove and let sit for 10 minutes, then serve.

NONNA IGEA'S TIPS

- If using fresh spinach, make sure you cook it in advance so you have time to drain the water. If it still has water in it and you mix this into the ricotta, it can make the cannelloni soggy.
- Drain the ricotta thoroughly to prevent excess moisture, or if possible, source a dry ricotta.
- When filling your crepes, don't put too much inside or you won't be able to close them properly. Test one first to check the amount you need.

RISOTTO AI FUNGHI MUSHROOM RISOTTO

For Vincenzo, cooking is about ingredients making love, and in this case, the union of mushrooms with creamy carnaroli rice creates a rich, velvety risotto – a classic culinary romance.

Vincenzo is well skilled when it comes to risotto, and he has taught me (and so many of you!) that it's not a dish to be afraid of. Making risotto is a gentle, slow process with just a few steps. The most significant of all is to 'just keep stirring'! Risotto's versatility allows it to be made with almost any vegetable or protein, so you can make it with pantry staples or get fancy with truffle and seafood. For this version, porcini mushrooms are the hero. Mixed mushrooms (or simply your favourites) are a perfect substitute. And yes, the final step of adding butter makes all the difference.

SERVES 4

½ cup (120ml/4 fl oz) extra virgin olive oil (EVOO)
400g (14.1 oz) fresh porcini mushrooms, sliced
pinch of salt
bunch of flat-leaf (Italian) parsley, leaves and stems chopped
½ brown onion, diced
300g (10.6 oz) carnaroli rice
½ glass white wine, preferably dry
1L (33.8 fl oz) vegetable stock, hot
50g (1.7 oz) butter
50g (1.7 oz) Parmigiano Reggiano, finely grated
freshly cracked black pepper
fresh truffle, grated (optional)

METHOD

1 Heat a large frying pan over medium-low heat and add half the EVOO. When the oil is slightly warm, add the mushroom. Using a wooden spoon, stir and simmer for a few minutes. Add a pinch of salt and half the parsley, then mix. Cook, stirring every few minutes, for 15 minutes, or until the mushroom is tender and glossy. Remove from heat and leave to the side.

2 To cook the rice, warm the remaining EVOO in a large saucepan or deep frying pan over medium-low heat. Add the onion and sauté for 10 minutes, or until it starts to soften, mixing it every so often with a wooden spoon. Don't rush this; be gentle.

3 When the onion is cooked, add the rice and stir. The rice needs to lightly toast in the pan for 4–5 minutes. Stir frequently. Add the wine and keep an eye on the time. From this point, cook according to the length of time on the packet instructions.

4 Stir the wine through. You have to keep the rice moist at all times, so once the wine evaporates, start adding the stock, one ladle at a time, mixing it in. Leave to reduce before adding another ladle of stock. The key: keep stirring during the entire process and do not increase the heat; the rice is best cooked gently and slowly. It will become beautiful and creamy during this process, so long as you add stock each time it dries up.

5 A few minutes before the recommended cooking time for the rice, add the cooked mushroom, reserving some for garnish. Add another ½ ladle of stock. Stir through, adding more stock as needed, because the mushroom will quickly absorb the liquid. Keep stirring and taste the rice to make sure it is cooked through.

6 Add the butter and Parmigiano and stir through. Keep stirring until both have melted and you get a creamy texture. To serve, ladle a portion into the centre of a large plate, then gently tap the bottom of the plate to spread it evenly (Vincenzo's signature trick). Top with the extra mushrooms, a sprinkle of Parmigiano, pepper, the remaining parsley and fresh truffle.

VINCENZO'S TIPS

- If you can't find fresh porcini mushrooms, use dried porcini mushrooms. Just rehydrate them in veggie stock or boiled water for 20–30 minutes before cooking. Use this liquid as part of the stock too, as it will add an intense flavour to the rice.
- Reheating leftovers? Add a touch of hot stock, butter and Parmigiano to the pan.

LASAGNA CLASSICA CLASSIC LASAGNA

By far, one of the most popular recipes Vincenzo has ever shared with his community is this traditional Italian lasagna. Across the regions of Italy, lasagna recipes vary, with more ingredients added the further south you go. But the original birthplace was Bologna, and the traditional dish features minimal ingredients and maximum flavour. If you've tried it, you know it's unbeatable. If not, your life is about to change. This cultural icon sparks endless debate: should it be plain or extra saucy, have more meat, or even peas and eggs (oops, guilty – I'm a third-generation Calabrese, and we enjoy these additions). This recipe keeps things traditional: layers of delicate pasta sheets, tender veal and pork mince in tomato sugo, freshly made *besciamella* and just the right amount of cheese, cooked to crispy-edged perfection. It's time to fight for your favourite piece – are you an edge-piece or middle-piece lasagna lover?

SERVES 6
extra virgin olive oil (EVOO), qb
1 carrot, diced
1 celery stalk, leaves removed, diced
½ brown onion, diced
500g (17.6 oz) minced (ground) veal
500g (17.6 oz) minced (ground) pork
1 glass red wine
2 × 700g (24.7 oz) bottles store-bought passata or use homemade (see recipe, page 74)
salt and pepper
500g fresh egg lasagna pasta sheets (about 2 packets, or 10–12 sheets)
Pecorino Romano or Parmigiano Reggiano, finely grated, qb
provolone, diced
2 fresh fior di latte or buffalo mozzarella balls, cubed
1 batch Besciamella sauce (see recipe, page 67)

METHOD

1 To make the ragù, add a generous amount of EVOO to a large saucepan and let it slowly heat over a medium–low heat. Add the carrot, celery, onion and cook for 5–10 minutes, or until the vegetables start to soften.

2 Add the mince, breaking it down into using a wooden spoon while it starts to brown. Simmer, stirring frequently, until it darkens and is cooked through. Stir in the wine and simmer until it evaporates, stirring occasionally and reducing the heat if necessary.

3 Pour 1½ bottles of passata over the mince mixture, season and cover. Simmer, stirring occasionally still over medium–low heat, for 1 hour. If it bubbles too much, lower the heat.

4 Take off the lid, add a glass of water (the passata should have reduced) and cook over low heat for another hour, stirring regularly.

5 Preheat the oven to 180°C (350°F). Using a pastry brush, line a deep glass baking dish or similar deep baking tray with EVOO.

6 Spread a scoop of sauce over the base of the prepared dish, then lay down the first layer of lasagna sheets, cutting them to size if need be.

7 Spread the ragù evenly over the pasta, then top with the 3 cheeses. Spread over a light layer of besciamella. Repeat layering with more pasta, ragù, cheeses and besciamella, aiming for 5–6 layers. Spread a final layer of ragù on top, covering the entire surface. Cover the lasagna with foil and bake for 20 minutes, or until the edges have started to turn golden and crispy but before the top dries up too much.

8 Remove from the oven and discard foil. Sprinkle with Pecorino or Parmigiano. Return to the oven, uncovered, for another 10 minutes then cool for 10 minutes before serving.

VINCENZO'S TIPS
- Put any leftover ragù in containers and store in the fridge for 2 days or in the freezer for up to 6 months.
- The best lasagna sheets are homemade, but store-bought ones are a convenient alternative. Some fresh sheets are pre-cooked, while others need a quick boil in salted water. Check the packet instructions first.
- Use ingredients in moderation when creating your layers and never add too much sauce as it can make the lasagna soggy and not so nice.

TIMBALLO ALLA TERAMANA DI NONNA IGEA
TRADITIONAL LASAGNA FROM TERAMO

You know that dish that means so much to you? The one you remember devouring alongside family while creating core childhood memories? The dish that brings you to your knees and makes your heart skip a beat? This is that dish for Vincenzo: Nonna Igea's pride and joy, the heart of her table and a symbol of the family being brought together. Layer upon layer of delicately handmade, thin crepes (no pasta sheets here) smothered in her tomato sugo, tender mince, juicy mozzarella and salty Parmigiano cheese. Some say lasagna, we say *timballo alla Teramana*.

It is difficult to describe how much this dish means to us. Nonna has been making timballo for more than 70 years, and has shared with us every last detail on how to recreate it. We can only hope that we have described it in such a way as to honour her. That is the epitome of what we seek to do at Vincenzo's Plate: share recipes and memories, and embrace the notion that there is not a lot else that compares to being brought together over a shared meal.

SERVES 12
extra virgin olive oil (EVOO), qb
600g (21.1 oz) minced (ground) pork and veal
pinch of salt
butter, qb
1 egg
50ml (2 oz) full-fat milk
30–35 freshly made crepes (see recipe, page 114)
3 fresh fior di latte or buffalo mozzarella balls, diced
1 batch Tomato and basil sugo, slightly cooled (see recipe, page 60)
200g (7 oz) Parmigiano Reggiano, finely grated, plus extra (optional), to serve

METHOD

1 Place a medium frying pan over medium heat and add a drizzle of EVOO. Once this warms up, add the mince, breaking it down with a fork, and sprinkle a pinch of salt on top. Let this cook for a few minutes, or until it browns, then set aside to cool.

2 Cut a cube of butter and use it to grease a large, deep baking tray or dish, rubbing it all over – don't miss the corners! This will prevent the *timballo* sticking as it cooks.

3 In a separate bowl, crack in the egg and whisk well. Add the milk and 2 pinches of salt and mix again.

4 Once the mince mixture has cooled, it's time to assemble the *timballo*. Preheat the oven to 180°C (360°F).

5 Line the bottom of the prepared tray or dish with some crepes. Then, line the sides of the tray with another set of crepes, laying each one so half of the crepe covers the side of the tray and the other half folds over the edge. Add as many crepes as you need to ensure there are no gaps. You might need to cut some to size, a little like a puzzle.

Continued on next page >

TIMBALLO ALLA TERAMANA DI NONNA IGEA
TRADITIONAL LASAGNA FROM TERAMO (CONT'D)

6 Scatter just under a third of the mozzarella cubes on top of the crepes, then add a few scoops of sugo, spreading gently with the back of a tablespoon. Don't add too much or the crepes will soften and the *timballo* might collapse. Add some mince mixture to this layer – sporadically and not too much – before mixing in a generous amount of grated Parmigiano.

7 Dip a remaining crepe into the egg mixture, then lift it to let all the excess mixture drip off. Lay this crepe on top of the mince layer, then dip another crepe into the egg mixture and repeat until the mince layer is covered with crepes.

8 Repeat steps 6 and 7, adding a few small cubes of butter on every second layer, until all your crepes are finished (or your *timballo* is so tall it is the height of the tray!) The butter helps keep the ingredients moist once cooking in the oven – this will add extra flavour too! Reserve any leftover egg mixture.

9 Now fold the crepes hanging over the edge back on top of the *timballo*, closing it up tightly. Using a large spoon, drizzle more sugo on top and spread it thinly – again, not too much. Add a few extra pieces of mozzarella on top. Using a thin, sharp knife make up to 6 slits down into the *timballo* and pour a small amount of the reserved egg mixture into each slit. This helps the *timballo* cook through and stay moist.

10 Cook in the oven for 1 hour, or until it is crisp on top and all the cheese is melted. Remove from the oven and allow it to cool and set for around 10 minutes. Then slice it into individual portions. There is no need to add any extra Parmigiano on top before serving, but some of us can't help it!

NONNA IGEA'S TIPS
- Be organised! Make all the elements ahead of time so when you need to assemble the *timballo*, you can create the layers with ease.
- Make extra crepes! It can be hard to estimate how many you need for the *timballo* as the size will vary according to the tray or dish you use, the size of your eggs and so on. Nonna suggests always making a few more so you don't find yourself at the end with gaps you're not able to cover.
- If you are lucky enough to have any leftover crepes, you can serve them as dessert, warmed slightly with melted chocolate, fresh berries or even honey drizzled on top. Then roll and share (or not – they might just be too good).
- There is no need to cook the meat for too long, as it will have more time to cook in the oven.
- You can assemble the *timballo* the day before you want to cook and serve it. Leave in the fridge covered with foil, then take it out while the oven preheats. Sometimes when I have a big occasion to prepare for, I'll make mine ahead and store it in the freezer – it'll store for up to 3 months. Just defrost it in the fridge 24–48 hours before you want to serve, then cook it in the oven once thawed.

PASTA CON BROCCOLI E RICOTTA RICOTTA AND BROCCOLI PASTA

This is a cherished recipe from Calabria, where my nonni are from. While nothing compares to the broccoli freshly picked from (my) Nonno Vincenzo's garden, the combination of this tender vegetable with creamy ricotta still makes it a family favourite.

It's a true one-pot wonder and every time we make it the aroma brings a flood of memories. Nonno always served his portion in an oversized salad bowl, and as a young girl I marvelled at how he devoured every last strand. His broccoli was never too soft, never too firm, and his pasta always al dente. Nonno loved this dish, and like clockwork, it was on the menu every time he had a chance to visit his favourite ricotta supplier. I vividly remember him arriving in the early hours of the morning, with warm, freshly made ricotta that we'd slather on crusty bread. It was at that point we knew we were having this dish for dinner.

SERVES 2–3
1 tbsp rock salt
300g (10.6 oz) spaghettoni or spaghetti pasta
500g (17.6 oz) broccoli, florets cut into pieces and stalk sliced, keeping some larger for blending later
extra virgin olive oil (EVOO), qb
200g (7 oz) ricotta
Pecorino Romano, finely grated, qb
1–2 garlic cloves, peeled and crushed
small bunch of basil

SPECIAL EQUIPMENT
immersion blender

METHOD

1 Bring a large pot of water to a rolling boil, add rock salt and allow to dissolve. Add the pasta, gently pushing down with tongs if necessary, then the broccoli too. Cook, stirring occasionally with a wooden spoon, for 5 minutes. Using a hand sieve, remove the larger broccoli pieces and stem (making sure they are tender) and transfer to a plate. Continue cooking the pasta and remaining broccoli for another 5 minutes, or until the pasta has finished cooking. By this stage the broccoli should be cooked through too. A few minutes before the pasta is ready, scoop up a mug of pasta water.

2 Meanwhile, make the sauce. In a blender, add the broccoli on the plate to the blender along with a generous pour of EVOO and a splash of pasta water. Blend until it starts to get a creamy consistency, adding more EVOO or pasta water depending on how thick you want the sauce.

3 In a bowl, combine the ricotta, a sprinkle of Pecorino and a splash of pasta water, mixing it together with a fork until it is smooth and creamy.

4 Heat a large frying pan over medium heat. Add a drizzle of EVOO and the garlic. Cook for 30 seconds before pouring in the blended broccoli cream and spread it out over the pan. Tear some basil leaves and add them to the pan. Pour in a small amount of pasta water to keep the broccoli cream from sticking or burning.

5 When the pasta is ready, use tongs to transfer it directly into the pan and don't worry if some pasta water drips in – after all, it is known as tears from the pasta gods! Combine everything in the pan using a wooden spoon. If too dry, add more pasta water.

6 Ensure the pasta is evenly coated with the creamy broccoli sauce and add a scoop of the ricotta mixture too. To serve, twirl the pasta onto serving plates using tongs. Dollop on more ricotta cream and garnish with more basil and Pecorino, obviously.

VINCENZO'S TIPS
- Don't get rid of any broccoli leaves! Cook these along with the rest of the broccoli as they add lots of nutrients and texture too.
- Feel free to adjust the amount of garlic. I prefer 1 clove, but garlic lovers (I know you're out there!) might want more.
- The secret to this dish is using high-quality ricotta. Skip the overly smooth, creamy types. What you need is ricotta that's slightly grainy, as it brings a better texture to your pasta.

CHITARRA ALLA TERAMANA
THE ORIGINAL SPAGHETTI AND MEATBALLS FROM TERAMO

This is the ultimate spaghetti and meatballs.

There's a lot to be said about the taste of that favourite dish you grew up eating. For Vincenzo, it's chitarra with mini meatballs (*polpettine*), made proudly by Nonna Igea. While recreating any favourite may seem like a challenge, it soon becomes your own – and just as loved.

When Nonna makes this, the aroma that wafts through the house and up the stairs to the apartments above, where all her family live, is something truly breathtaking and irresistible. For us, this is one of her signature dishes, a recipe the whole family has learnt how to cook, to make her proud and to make sure it is never forgotten.

As the artisan of this hearty dish, she claims there are not a lot of secrets behind it, other than her experience, patience and, you guessed it, quality ingredients! It's a staple at Sunday lunches and family gatherings, and when her grandchildren crave it, she never says no. Even the youngest members of our family fell in love with this dish – Sebastian at just 20 months old and his brother even earlier, at 10 months!

We have carefully detailed Nonna's steps to getting this dish right, and know you will honour her by doing your best to follow them. While many think of spaghetti and meatballs as a serving of long pasta with large meatballs, that is something created outside Italy and isn't traditional. This, on the other hand, is from Nonna's region of Teramo in Abruzzo, and it's a masterpiece.

SERVES 5
1 batch Tomato and basil sugo (see recipe, page 60)
1 tbsp rock salt
500g (17.6 oz) spaghetti alla chitarra (to make Nonna Igea's incredible fresh version, see recipe, page 91, or use store-bought spaghetti quadrati pasta)
Parmigiano Reggiano, finely grated

POLPETTINE (MINI MEATBALLS)
300g (10.6 oz) minced (ground) veal
1 egg yolk
2 tbsp finely grated Parmigiano Reggiano
salt
extra virgin olive oil (EVOO), qb

METHOD

1 To make the polpettine, place the veal and egg yolk in a bowl. Mix well using a fork. Add the Parmigiano and a sprinkle of salt and mix through using your hands. Squash down into the mixture with your fingers, letting the ingredients combine.

2 Drizzle EVOO on a small plate, then dip two fingers in and rub them onto the palm of one hand – this will prevent the mince from sticking to your hands when forming the mini meatballs.

3 Take a small portion of the mince mixture, place it on one hand, then roll it between your palms to create a tiny ball. Place on a large, flat plate.

4 Repeat steps 2 and 3 until you use up all the mince mixture.

5 Bring a small saucepan of water to the boil, then add the meatballs and cook for no more than 1–2 minutes – Nonna is efficient! Using a large, slotted spoon, transfer the mini meatballs onto a plate to rest. (You can also lightly fry the mini meatballs in a small amount of EVOO – and they are even tastier, but when Nonna prepares for a large group with children as guests too, she prefers to boil them.)

Continued on next page >

CHITARRA ALLA TERAMANA
THE ORIGINAL SPAGHETTI AND MEATBALLS FROM TERAMO (CONT'D)

6 Place a small saucepan over low heat. Pour in a large scoop of sugo, before adding the mini meatballs and mix through the sauce. Cook for 10 minutes, or until the meatballs are cooked through and immersed in the sugo.

7 Bring a large pot of water to a rolling boil, add rock salt and allow to dissolve. Add the pasta and cook for about 3–5 minutes, tasting it for your desired texture – but don't overdo it. Every so often, mix the pasta so the strands don't stick together.

8 Add a ladle of sugo to a large serving bowl. Drain the pasta and transfer it to the bowl, then mix in another generous scoop of sugo and plenty of cheese using a large fork or wooden spoon. Add more sugo as needed to coat the pasta evenly.

9 Add a large portion of the mini meatballs to the bowl and mix gently, setting some aside to garnish each serve. For plating, add a spoonful of sugo to the base of each plate, then use tongs to plate the pasta. Top with the extra meatballs, sugo and a final sprinkle of cheese. Egg pasta absorbs sugo quickly, so be generous to keep the dish moist. Offer additional cheese at the table for serving.

NONNA IGEA'S TIPS
- Spend the time you need to create these mini meatballs. When you scoop them up with your strands of pasta smothered in sauce, it will all be worth it as you taste every flavour in the same bite.
- The mini meatballs are pre-cooked so that you don't add them raw into the sauce. This prevents them from breaking or overcooking – they should be tender to bite, so don't cook any longer than necessary.

RISOTTO ALLA MILANESE SAFFRON RISOTTO

Risotto alla Milanese is a classic Italian dish that embodies simplicity with a touch of luxury. While rice dishes might seem like humble peasant food, the addition of saffron elevates this one to new heights of decadence – making it a true blend of *cucina povera* and gourmet.

Saffron is one of the most expensive ingredients in Italian cooking, mainly as a result of its labour-intensive harvesting process. To transform a dish from simple to an explosion of flavours, you really only need a few pinches of saffron, and this recipe is no different. It requires no additional garnish – although, yes, we always add grated Pecorino! When properly prepared, the risotto emits the irresistible aroma of saffron and boasts a creamy, sunflower-yellow sauce, which suspends each grain of rice perfectly. Served warm, it should spread out easily and flow gently, with the texture neither too thin nor clumpy.

SERVES 4

1 tsp saffron strands, plus extra for garnishing (optional)
½ cup (125ml/4.2 fl oz) boiling water
2 cups (500ml/16.9 fl oz) beef stock
80g (2.8 oz) butter
½ brown onion, finely diced
200g (7 oz) carnaroli rice
1 glass white wine
salt and pepper
3–4 tbsp finely grated Parmigiano Reggiano

METHOD

1 In a small bowl, pour the boiling water over the saffron, stirring until the water turns golden. Cover and let sit as long as possible (see tips).

2 Gently bring the stock to the boil in a medium saucepan over medium heat. It needs to be hot when you add it to the rice.

3 Meanwhile, place a frying pan over medium heat and add half the butter along with the onion and sauté, stirring with a wooden spoon, for 3–5 minutes, or until the mixture becomes creamy and the onion softens. Add the rice and toast for 4–5 minutes, then pour in the wine. This marks the start of the cooking process for the rice. Follow the packet instructions to determine the amount of time the rice now needs to cook for.

4 While cooking, stir the rice continuously, and as it starts to dry up, add a ladle full of hot stock. As the mixture reduces, continue adding more stock to make sure it never dries out and the rice is always wet. Keep adding stock until about 2–3 minutes before the rice is ready (per the cooking time instructions). At this point, add the saffron liquid to the pan. Continue to cook and stir for the remaining few minutes while the saffron turns the rice a beautiful shade of yellow.

5 Season with salt and pepper, mix, then remove from the heat and add the Parmigiano and remaining butter right away, stirring quickly so everything dissolves and combines well.

6 Toss well to combine and thicken the risotto, but if you aren't brave enough, simply mix continuously until the texture is creamy. To serve, scoop a portion of your risotto into the centre of each plate. Gently tap the bottom of the plate with the palm of your hand to spread the risotto across the entire surface. Garnish with strands of saffron.

VINCENZO'S TIPS

- If you plan ahead, dissolve your saffron in a glass of freshly boiled water in the morning before you plan to make this dish for dinner (or even for up to 2 days before using it). Cover it (and maybe label it, so no one drinks it!) and let it sit until you're ready to cook. Even if you don't do this, the saffron will still make your risotto delicious, it will simply be less concentrated.
- You know I'm a lover of EVOO, and if you prefer it instead of butter, you can use it, but don't expect the same creamy texture – you heard it from me!

SPAGHETTI AL POMODORO

If you have some cherry tomatoes and pasta on hand, as well as 15 minutes, then there is no excuse not to make this dish! It never fails. When we don't know what to make for dinner, this normally takes centre stage. It makes us pretty nostalgic, as both our families love cooking this for a meal or when last-minute guests show up.

How it took until the late 1700s for pasta to be mixed with tomatoes, I'll never know, but it's a marriage like no other and there is nothing that can break this bond. I mean, can you imagine never having tasted the culinary delight that is pasta smothered in tomato?

SERVES 3
1 tbsp rock salt
3 tbsp extra virgin olive oil (EVOO), plus extra for topping
2 garlic cloves, crushed
400g (14.1 oz) cherry tomatoes, halved, vines removed
salt and pepper
small bunch of basil
300g (10.6 oz) spaghetti quadrati pasta (thick spaghetti)
Pecorino Romano, finely grated (optional but always necessary if you're Vincenzo!), qb

METHOD

1 Bring a large pot of water to a rolling boil, add rock salt, and allow to dissolve.

2 While waiting for the water to boil, prepare your sauce. Heat a generous drizzle of EVOO in a large frying pan over medium–low heat, then add the garlic. Cook for about 30 seconds, and if it starts to burn, add a splash of water. Add the tomato, then season with salt and pepper. Cook, stirring frequently with a wooden spoon, until the tomato softens and the juices start to seep out.

3 Break off 2 basil sprigs (stems included!) from the bunch of basil and add to the frying pan, then stir to infuse the flavours. After 10 minutes, you should have a pan full of juices. Remove the basil, transfer the mixture to a blender and pulse for 5 seconds. It is essential you do this gently and fast.

4 Now add the pasta to the boiling water. For al dente pasta, cook it for 2 minutes less than in the packet instructions.

5 While the pasta is cooking, pour the blended sauce back into the frying pan. Heat over low heat for a few minutes, stirring occasionally and breaking the remaining basil leaves into small pieces and adding some to the sauce. Reserve a few (better looking ones) for the garnish.

6 Just before the pasta is ready, scoop up a mug of pasta water and leave to the side. Use tongs to transfer the pasta into the frying pan – even better if some water falls in. Mix through, ensuring the sauce evenly coats the pasta. Add a small amount of reserved pasta water to the pan. Toss if you can, otherwise mix through until it thickens the sauce.

7 Once each strand is lathered in the sauce, add a final drizzle of EVOO and some of the reserved basil leaves, whole or torn. Use tongs to pull up the perfect portion of creamy, sauce-covered spaghetti and place it in the middle of a flat plate or serving bowl. Top the pasta with a spoonful of sauce from the pan and choose whether to add more basil. If you can't get enough of cheese, add some freshly grated Pecorino on top.

VINCENZO'S TIPS
- If you're using a garlic press or crusher, don't forget to scrape the bottom!
- Use a 400g (14.1 oz) canned whole peeled Italian tomatoes instead of cherry tomatoes, if you like. You can also use Parmigiano Reggiano if you don't have Pecorino.
- When cooking the tomato, help the juices come out by pressing down gently on each half with a spoon once they have started to soften. Be gentle with the skin – it's the secret ingredient for a creamier sauce.
- Avoid chopping the basil – just tear it up with your hands or add it in whole.

PASTA ALLA NORMA

Eggplants (aubergines) are a southern Italian staple, especially abundant in the warmer months. In the Vincenzo's Plate household, they are a favourite for their versatility and the textures they bring to every dish. This Sicilian recipe features thin, almost chip-like strips of eggplant, fried to a golden crunch. Paired with a rich tomato sauce and a garnish of ricotta salata, it's a classic combination.

An interesting fact: Pasta alla Norma is named after Bellini's 19th-century opera *Norma*. Once you try this dish, you might find yourself singing your way back to the pan for more! For those who follow us on social media or have joined one of our tours, you've likely heard Vincenzo belt out a tune or two. With his enthusiasm, you'd be forgiven for assuming his voice matches his cooking skills – but let's just say the kitchen is where he truly shines!

SERVES 4–6

- vegetable or sunflower oil, for frying
- 2 medium eggplants (aubergines) or 1 large
- 2 × 400g (14.1 oz) canned whole peeled Italian tomatoes
- extra virgin olive oil (EVOO), qb
- 2 garlic cloves, crushed
- salt and pepper
- small bunch of basil
- 1 tbsp rock salt
- 500g (17.6 oz) casarecce or penne rigate pasta
- 400g (14.1 oz) ricotta salata or Pecorino Sardo

METHOD

1 Pour vegetable or sunflower oil halfway up the side of a deep frying pan or small saucepan and heat to 180°C (360°F). Check the temperature using a food thermometer or by slightly dipping the bottom of a wooden spoon in the oil. If it bubbles up, it's ready.

2 While waiting for the oil to heat up, trim the top and bottom of each eggplant, then cut into 1cm (0.4 in) rounds, then strips.

3 Once the oil reaches the right temperature, fry a handful of eggplant strips. Move them around gently and after just 2 minutes, or when they start to turn golden brown, remove from the oil using a slotted spoon or small sieve and transfer to a plate lined with paper towel to absorb excess oil. Repeat with the remaining eggplant. If the strips start to burn, reduce the heat.

4 Crush the tomatoes in a bowl with a potato masher until they have broken down and created a thick, slightly clumpy mixture. Heat a generous drizzle of EVOO in a frying pan over medium–low heat. Add garlic and 2 tbsp water. Cook until lightly golden (30–40 seconds). Stir in the tomato, reduce to a simmer and cook for 20 minutes, pressing down on any large chunks. Season with salt and pepper. Mix in half the eggplant, then remove from heat. Tear some of the basil leaves, reserving a few for garnishing, and stir gently into the sauce and let rest.

5 Bring a large pot of water to a rolling boil, add rock salt, allow to dissolve and then cook your pasta according to the packet instructions. Once al dente, reserve a mug of pasta water then drain the pasta.

6 If the sauce has cooled, reheat over low heat. Add the pasta to the pan. Stir in at least half the reserved pasta water and cook for another minute, tossing as the sauce thickens. Grate most of the cheese over the pasta, mixing until melted. Serve in bowls or plates, topping with the remaining eggplant, extra grated cheese and a couple of basil leaves.

VINCENZO'S TIPS

- Don't cut the eggplant strips too thin or they'll burn when fried. If you're unsure, make them thicker and cook a little longer. For a crispier result, lightly dust with plain (all-purpose) flour before frying.
- You can substitute the peeled tomatoes with a bottle of tomato passata. The dish might not be as bold and fresh, but it will still taste delicious.
- If you can't find ricotta salata, substitute Pecorino Sardo – just make sure you grate it using a grater with larger holes so the pieces are thick and the flavour is beautifully salty. No, it won't be the same, but I promise you will still love it.

PAPPARDELLE AL RAGÙ DI CINGHIALE
PAPPARDELLE WITH WILD BOAR SAUCE

You can't truly appreciate the depth of flavour in this dish until your first bite. Vincenzo's papà, Paolo, is the expert behind this wild boar sauce, served only one way: over thick, fresh pappardelle pasta. The sauce clings to every ribbon, creating a hearty, unforgettable meal.

Wild boar has a robust, earthy flavour that's bold and delicious. It is also higher in protein and lower in saturated fat than other meats. When Vincenzo finds wild boar locally, it's cause for celebration. One bite of this dish and we're transported to Abruzzo, reminding us of gatherings at the outdoor dining table, with friends and family, being served by Paolo in all his glory (he loves to entertain, possibly even more than Vincenzo!).

SERVES 20

2kg (70.5 oz) wild boar meat, diced into chunks (source from a trusted butcher)
4 cups (1L/33.8 fl oz) red wine
6 fresh or dried bay leaves
pepper
small bunch of oregano
2 carrots, each cut into three pieces
1 onion, halved
extra virgin olive oil (EVOO), qb
1 glass white wine
5L (169 fl oz) or about 7 bottles store-bought passata or use homemade (see recipe, page 74)
1 celery stalk, with leaves intact
2 tbsp rock salt
1kg (35.3 oz) pappardelle pasta (see recipe, page 80, or buy high-quality dried pasta)
Pecorino Romano or Parmigiano Reggiano, finely grated, qb
crusty bread, to serve (optional)

METHOD

1 In a very large bowl, mix the boar, wine, bay leaves, pepper, oregano, 1 carrot and 1 onion half. Massage gently using both hands for a few minutes, then cover and marinate in the fridge for between 24–36 hours.

2 Remove the marinated boar from the fridge and carefully rinse each piece, discarding the herbs and vegetables. Heat a very large pot or Dutch oven over medium heat. Add a generous amount of EVOO. Once warm, carefully add the boar, searing all over.

3 After 10 minutes, add the remaining carrot and onion (roughly chopped), and move the meat around, making sure it doesn't stick to the bottom of the pan. Cook with the lid on, stirring occasionally, for a further 15–20 minutes. If it looks dry, reduce the heat slightly and add a touch more EVOO. Add the wine and leave to simmer. Once the vegetables are tender and the wine starts to evaporate, mix in the passata, then add the celery and half the salt. Reduce heat to very low. Simmer, stirring now and then, for up to 6 hours.

4 Remove pan from heat. Remove the celery. The boar should have broken down and softened completely. Mix gently so the meat tears and the sauce is filled with the shredded meat and some small chunks too.

5 When you are ready to serve, bring a large pot of water to a rolling boil, add rock salt, allow to dissolve and then cook your pasta. If using dry packet or fresh egg pasta, the cooking time will vary, so check the packet instructions, or for fresh, cook for 3 minutes, then taste.

6 Warm up half the ragù in a large frying pan. Strain and add the pasta – letting a touch of pasta water drop in when you transfer it to combine the pasta and ragù well. Turn off the heat. Ladle more ragù over the pasta, ensuring even coverage, then mix or toss to combine. Garnish with cheese and serve immediately with crusty bread to scoop up any leftover sauce (a practice known as *scarpetta* – if you know, you know!).

PAPÀ PAOLO'S TIPS
- This serving is quite large. Halve (or even quarter) it if you aren't cooking for 20 guests or make it all and freeze it in batches in airtight containers. It'll keep for up to 6 months.
- Check and stir the ragù occasionally to prevent sticking and ensure even cooking. This also helps to more fully integrate the flavours throughout the sauce.

PASTA E FAGIOLI DI NONNA IGEA PASTA WITH BEANS

No Italian household is complete without a family recipe for pasta with *fagioli* (beans). It is the epitome of *cucina povera*, transforming humble ingredients into a dish of immense comfort. While many people make it when pantry supplies are low, gourmet variations have started to surface in Italian restaurants. I wonder what our *bisnonni* would say today if they knew how much some are charging for a bowl!

Nonna Igea's original recipe calls for a specialty egg dough pasta known as *sagne*. This pasta starts as an extra-large sheet rolled out with a rolling pin, which is then cut into long lengths and even smaller strips. We wanted to make this version more accessible – something Nonna might whip up midweek. So we swapped the *sagne* for the more common pasta *ditali*.

For Nonna, this dish is a poignant reminder of her youth, when there was little else to eat and it was all they could afford. Yet, she still insists it's one of her favourite meals. Isn't it amazing how something others might view as a hardship can actually become a source of our fondest memories?

SERVES 4–6

- 400g (14.1 oz) dried cannellini or mixed beans (use any variety of dried beans that you prefer)
- 2 tsp salt
- extra virgin olive oil (EVOO), qb
- ¼ onion, diced
- ½ carrot, peeled and diced
- 700g (24.7 oz) bottle store-bought passata or use homemade (see recipe, page 74)
- 1 celery stalk
- handul of basil leaves
- 1 tbsp rock salt
- 400g (14.1 oz) ditali pasta
- Pecorino Romano or Parmigiano Reggiano, finely grated (optional), qb
- dried chilli flakes (optional)

METHOD

1 Rinse the beans well using a colander, then transfer them to a saucepan. Fill with cold water, making sure the water just covers the beans. Add 1 tsp salt, then boil over medium heat for 20–30 minutes, or until soft. Stir every so often to avoid them burning or becoming mushy.

2 For the sugo, place a medium saucepan over medium–low heat, then add the onion, carrot and a generous pour of EVOO. Sauté the soffritto until the vegetables soften, then add the passata, celery and 1 tsp salt. Add the basil leaves, then mix using a wooden spoon and cook for 20 minutes, stirring occasionally.

3 In the meantime, bring a large pot of water to a rolling boil, add rock salt, and allow to dissolve.

4 Once the sauce is ready, add a ladle full of it to the beans. This will create a soupy texture and the beans will start to absorb the flavour.

5 Cook the pasta according to the packet instructions. Once the pasta is ready, drain and portion into bowls before adding the bean mixture (your desired amount) using a ladle. To create a thicker texture, add 1–2 tbsp of the plain sugo and mix it through. Sprinkle some cheese on top and, if you like a hint of spice, some chilli. If you have good-quality EVOO, add a drizzle to each bowl for the perfect finishing touch.

NONNA IGEA'S TIPS

- You can use a variety of beans. Nonna prefers the white variety, borlotti beans, but you can even use a combination.
- While you can use packet pasta, if you have the time to make it fresh, do it and enjoy the dish as if you were in Nonna's kitchen.
- You will likely have some sugo left over. Use it the next day as a pasta sauce, or store it in an airtight container in the freezer for up to 6 months.

PASTA CA MUDDICA SPAGHETTI WITH BREADCRUMBS

In Nonna's kitchen nothing ever goes to waste, especially bread. Leftover bread has many uses and one of our favourite things to do with it is blitz it to make fresh breadcrumbs – which are the key to perfecting this pasta recipe. If you have yet to try this, go for it. You will never buy breadcrumbs again – as in, ever. You will also then fully understand how impactful this recipe is. If you use store-bought breadcrumbs, don't bother making this; it simply won't be the same. Or at least don't tell us …

This Sicilian recipe requires hardly any fuss, and the combination of the crunchy crumb, al dente pasta and hint of chilli is so satisfying you will wish you'd made more. In case you hadn't noticed, Vincenzo adores Pecorino, but this crumb is a great replacement – you can also use it as a topping on other dishes.

SERVES 2

3–4 slices stale bread (2–3 day old sourdough or Italian crusty bread is best), roughly chopped
1 tbsp rock salt
extra virgin olive oil (EVOO), qb
1 garlic clove, crushed
1 tsp dried chilli flakes, or more if desired
small bunch of flat-leaf (Italian) parsley, leaves chopped
300g (10.6 oz) spaghetti pasta
3 tbsp finely grated Pecorino Romano

METHOD

1 Blend the bread using a blender until it forms into thicker than standard breadcrumbs.

2 Bring a large pot of water to a rolling boil, add rock salt, and allow to dissolve.

3 Meanwhile, pour 6–8 tbsp EVOO into a frying pan over medium heat, before adding the garlic. Cook for 30 seconds, then add the breadcrumbs and stir with a wooden spoon to absorb the oil and toast until crunchy. If it dries out, add an extra drizzle of EVOO. When the crumbs are nearly crisp, stir in the chilli and half the parsley. Continue stirring until the mixture is golden brown and crunchy – this step is key, so take your time and avoid increasing the heat. Once the texture is right, remove from heat and transfer to a bowl.

4 Cook the spaghetti according to the packet instructions and, when it's almost ready, reserve a mug of pasta water. Drain the pasta, then add it to the pan used for the breadcrumbs. Add ¼ cup (60ml/2 fl oz) EVOO and warm over low heat. Pour half the reserved pasta water over the top, sprinkle with more parsley and mix well using tongs, or, if you can, toss until the water is absorbed. If it looks dry, add a bit more pasta water.

5 Remove the pan from heat and add the Pecorino, mixing it through really well or toss if you can manage. This will add a nice creaminess to your dish, but is a slight stray from the traditional version. (Keep it out if you prefer.)

6 Plate the pasta and sprinkle generously with the toasted breadcrumbs. For extra spice, add more chili. Serve immediately, as the pasta will absorb the oil (and dry out) if left too long. Add a drizzle of EVOO if needed or leave the EVOO bottle on the table for guests. Garnish with any remaining chopped parsley.

VINCENZO'S TIPS

- Don't rush or have the heat up too high when toasting the breadcrumbs. Stir the mixture regularly while cooking and leave until you get a really crispy result.
- If you make extra toasted breadcrumbs, they can be stored in the fridge in an airtight container for up to 1 month or stored uncooked in an airtight container in the freezer for up to 6 months. They don't even need to be defrosted; just add a portion straight to your pan. If using them as a crumb coating, spread them out on a baking tray and leave to defrost overnight.
- For an extra burst of salty richness, consider adding chopped anchovies.

PENNE ALL'ARRABBIATA

This classic Roman pasta is famous for its fiery sauce of tomatoes, olive oil, garlic and hot red chillies. While *arrabbiata* translates to 'angry', we think the heat delivers a joyous burst of flavour that dances on your tastebuds, which couldn't be more opposite to the name itself!

This recipe is simple to make and best paired with short pasta; the only question is: how much heat can you handle? It's a great dish to test your chilli tolerance, and Vincenzo's parents along with my papà see it as a competition: how much chilli is too much? For Vincenzo and me, not so much! Though I suddenly craved chilli while pregnant with Sebastian, which was as surprising as it was delightful, as we are not the biggest lovers of lots of heat. Ready in under 30 minutes, this dish delivers happiness far beyond its spicy reputation, so don't be fooled by the name!

SERVES 3–4

- 2 × 400g (14.1 oz) canned whole peeled Italian tomatoes
- extra virgin olive oil (EVOO), qb
- 3 garlic cloves, crushed
- 2 hot red chillies, finely chopped, more or less as desired
- salt and pepper
- small bunch of flat-leaf (Italian) parsley, leaves and stems chopped
- 1 tbsp rock salt
- 400g (14.1 oz) penne pasta
- finely grated Pecorino Romano, to serve (optional)

METHOD

1 Pour the tomatoes into a bowl and crush them either by hand or using a potato masher, breaking them down and helping to release lots of tomato juices.

2 Add a generous amount of EVOO to a large frying pan and warm over medium heat. Add the garlic along with a splash of water to prevent it from burning. Cook, stirring occasionally, until slightly golden. Add the chilli – as much or as little as you like.

3 Pour the crushed tomatoes into the pan and cook for 5 minutes. Press down on the tomatoes a few more times using the potato masher to really thicken the sauce. Continue to allow the juices to ooze out. Cook for 15 minutes, then season generously with salt and pepper, before adding most of the parsley, reserving some for garnishing. Give it a final mix to combine, then turn off the heat.

4 Bring a large pot of water to a rolling boil, add rock salt, allow to dissolve and then cook your pasta according to the packet instructions. Once al dente, reserve a mug of pasta water then drain the pasta.

5 Add the pasta to the pan. Mix in 2–3 tbsp of the reserved pasta water, tossing to thicken the sauce. Top with parsley and more chilli, if you can handle it. Plate the pasta, adding Pecorino, if using, and any remaining parsley and chilli and the sugo from the pan.

VINCENZO'S TIPS
- There really isn't a lot to getting this recipe right, so please, I'm begging you, spend time sourcing quality ingredients and this will guarantee an authentic flavour.
- The best part about this dish is you can personalise it with as much or as little chilli, Pecorino and parsley as you like. Even though chilli isn't my favourite, when I make this dish I always try to add extra to see how much I can handle!
- For a milder dish, remove the seeds and white pith from the chillies; if you prefer more heat, include these to intensify the spiciness.

SPAGHETTI ALLA PARMIGIANA
SPAGHETTI WITH EGGPLANT IN TOMATO SAUCE

Another Calabrese classic on high rotation in our house is this incredibly satisfying eggplant pasta. This recipe has been in my family for as long as I can remember and is a personal favourite, and one of my mum's specialties. Thankfully, she has entrusted us with her instructions and all-important secrets, so you can make my childhood favourite for your family too. The flavour of the eggplant melds with tomato sugo, cheese and fresh breadcrumbs, creating a combination reminiscent of a traditional parmigiana, but with the delightful addition of pasta. Whoever thought of this deserves a medal. Yum.

SERVES 4–6

3 large eggplants (aubergines), peeled, skins discarded
salt and pepper
210g (7.4 oz) finely chopped tomatoes
700g (24.7 oz) bottle store-bought passata or use homemade (see recipe, page 74)
extra virgin olive oil (EVOO), qb
1 brown or red onion, diced
4 garlic cloves, diced
dried chilli flakes (optional)
large handful of basil leaves, torn
1 tbsp rock salt
500g (17.6 oz) spaghetti (it's also scrumptious served with short pasta varieties)
4 heaped tbsp finely grated Pecorino Romano
4 heaped tbsp homemade breadcrumbs (see tips)

METHOD

1 Halve each eggplant, then slice into 1cm (½ inch) thick strips. Place the strips in a colander, sprinkle generously with salt, and toss with your hands to mix. Place a large plate on top of the colander (facing down) so it sits directly on top of and touches the eggplant. Set the colander in a large bowl, then put a weight (for example, my mum uses a kettle filled with water, but cans also work) on top of the plate and leave to the side.

2 Combine the tomatoes and passata in a bowl. Heat a large pot over medium heat. Drizzle generously with EVOO. Add the onion and half the garlic, stirring with a wooden spoon, until golden. Season with pepper and optional chilli, then pour in the tomato mixture and add 1 tsp salt. Stir well. Simmer over low heat, stirring occasionally, for 30 minutes.

3 While the sauce is cooking, lift the weights and plate off the eggplant and remove the bowl from underneath. Squeeze a handful of eggplant at a time over the bowl or your kitchen sink to remove excess water, then transfer to a separate, clean bowl.

4 Heat a medium saucepan over low heat, drizzle generously with EVOO, then add the remaining garlic. Stir until it sizzles gently. Add the eggplant and simmer for 5 minutes, or until softened. Season with pepper and optional chilli, then add basil leaves, reserving a few. Test for tenderness with a fork, and once ready, remove from heat. Add the eggplant to the sauce, mix well and cook, stirring occasionally, for 15–20 minutes.

5 Bring a large pot of water to a rolling boil, add rock salt, allow to dissolve and then cook your pasta according to the packet instructions. While the pasta is cooking, mix the Pecorino and breadcrumbs in a bowl.

6 Add a few reserved basil leaves to the sauce, then three-quarters of the Pecorino mixture. Cover and simmer while you drain the pasta using a colander.

7 Add 2 scoops of sauce to the pot where you cooked your pasta, layering half of the pasta on top. Add more sauce, the rest of the pasta and cover again with more sauce.

MAMMA MARIA'S TIPS
- This pasta requires tender eggplants. If you find smaller ones that are tender, buy a large quantity to compensate for their size.
- To make homemade breadcrumbs, simply blend slightly stale bread down to a crumb.
- Freeze any leftovers in airtight containers for up to 6 months. You can also use it to make a pasta bake, or serve atop charred bread as a bruschetta – this is hard to beat!

PASTA AL FORNO BAKED PASTA

Pasta al forno is beloved across Italy, with variations by region – and even by town! This classic version combines pasta, tomato sugo, fresh mozzarella, provolone, grated Pecorino and our favourite additions. Growing up, we always had it with *prosciutto cotto* (ham) and boiled egg, a common variation in Calabria. Vincenzo's favourite ingredients to add, on the other hand, are mortadella or salami. We definitely argue over what tastes better, but it ends up coming down to who is in the kitchen making it!

It's also perfect for using leftover pasta. Just mix with your favourite ingredients and bake until the edges are crisp and golden, and the mozzarella is perfectly melted. Pro tip: undercook the pasta slightly, don't overload with sugo and be generous with the cheese!

SERVES 6

- 60–80ml (2–2.7 fl oz) extra virgin olive oil (EVOO), plus extra for frying and drizzling
- ½ brown onion, diced
- 2 × 700g (24.7 oz) bottles store-bought passata or use homemade (see recipe, page 74)
- rock salt
- 500g (17.6 oz) minced (ground) pork and veal
- small bunch of basil
- 3 eggs
- 500g (17.6 oz) rigatoni pasta
- 1 dry or fresh fior di latte ball, diced
- 1 large ball fresh buffalo mozzarella, diced
- 100g (3.5 oz) Pecorino Romano, finely grated
- 150–200g Calabrese spicy salami, chopped
- 50g (1.7 oz) provolone, diced

METHOD

1 Heat the EVOO in a large saucepan over medium heat. Add the onion and sauté for 6–7 minutes, or until golden. Stir in the passata, bring to a simmer and season with salt. Cover and cook for 30 minutes, stirring occasionally.

2 Meanwhile, heat EVOO in a frying pan. Add the mince, breaking it into small pieces with a wooden spoon. Cover and cook for 6–8 minutes, stirring after 5 minutes, or until browned and cooked through. Remove from heat.

3 Once the tomato sauce is ready, remove the lid and stir in the basil leaves. Add two ladles of the sauce to the mince and combine.

4 Meanwhile, bring a large pot of water to the boil. Add 1 tbsp rock salt and allow to dissolve. In a separate saucepan, boil the eggs for 12–14 minutes, then transfer to a bowl of iced water. Cook the pasta, draining it 3 minutes before the recommended cooking time.

5 Add the pasta to the sauce and mix well, but be gentle so the pasta doesn't break. Peel and slice the boiled eggs, then set aside.

6 Preheat the oven to 180°C (360°F).

7 To assemble, spread a layer of sauce over the base of a baking dish, followed by some of the pasta, mince mixture, fior di latte, mozzarella, Pecorino, salami and egg. Repeat layering, finishing with egg. Scatter the provolone over the top. Place in the oven, checking after 20 minutes. If not browned around the edges, bake for another 10–15 minutes.

8 Cool for 5 minutes to avoid it breaking up too much as you plate it up. Cut into portions using a slotted spatula or knife and serve on flat plates. Pasta al forno tastes amazing (arguably better) the next day. Just reheat in a pan with a drizzle of EVOO until crispy.

VINCENZO'S TIPS

- It's all about the prep. Cut up all your ingredients before starting and make the sauce ahead. If this is all done beforehand, it means I'm even closer to eating!
- The ideal pasta for this dish is rigatoni, which offers the best crispy texture on top when baked; however, ziti or conchiglioni are also great substitutions.
- Try not to fight over the corner pieces when serving, especially if you get the crunchy result we are after. Lucky for me, Suzanne prefers the middle section, so I get to enjoy the crispy edges every single time.

POLENTA AL SUGO CON LA SALSICCIA
POLENTA WITH TOMATO SAUCE AND SAUSAGES

Little compares to Nonna Igea's warm, creamy polenta on a cold day, especially when it's topped with her rich *salsiccia* (sausage) sugo. While polenta traditionally hails from northern Italy, it's been embraced across the country for generations. In Abruzzo, every family has their own recipe, as it is also a commonly served dish. However, this version isn't as widely known, which is a shame because it's beyond delicious.

Picture a long wooden board placed at the centre of the table, the golden polenta spread across it. The texture is soft but not wobbly, and there are spoons aplenty, ready for everyone to dig in and devour – this experience is a true celebration of Italian communal dining. For me, this dish transports me instantly to a Sunday meal at Nonna's house. Even in the heat of summer, I can't leave without asking her to make it. When this simmers away, the mouthwatering aroma fills the air, evoking the feeling that Nonna is right there with you, sharing her love and tradition. Succulent sausage sugo over velvety polenta is pure Italian comfort.

SERVES 4–6

extra virgin olive oil (EVOO), qb
1/2 carrot, diced
1/2 onion, diced
300g (10.6 oz) minced (ground) pork
2 pork ribs
4 pork sausages
rock salt
700g (24.7 oz) bottle store-bought passata or use homemade (see recipe, page 74)
100g (3.5 oz) pancetta, diced
250g (8.8 oz) polenta (or top quality cornmeal)
finely grated Parmigiano Reggiano, to serve

METHOD

1 Add a generous amount of EVOO to a medium saucepan and heat over medium–low heat. Add the carrot and onion. Simmer for 1–2 minutes, stirring with a wooden spoon.

2 Add the mince, ribs and 1 sausage, breaking up the mince as it cooks. Drizzle with EVOO, stir occasionally and cook until browned. Season with salt. Add the passata and simmer for at least 1 hour, or until the meat is tender and the sauce has reduced.

3 While the sugo is cooking, add a drizzle of EVOO to a frying pan and warm it up over medium–high heat. Remove the casing from the remaining sausages and break them down using a fork. Reduce to medium–low heat and cook until well browned, then add the pancetta and a pinch of salt. Mix thoroughly with the wooden spoon and ensure it has started to become crispy – but not burnt – then remove from heat.

4 Fill a large pot with 4 cups (1L/33.8 fl oz) water and leave it to heat up, but don't boil it! Once it is hot, add a pinch of rock salt, then gradually sprinkle in the polenta, stirring continuously with a wooden spoon. Avoid adding it all at once – let it expand and thicken as you mix. After 10 minutes (or when you see the polenta start to thicken), use a ladle to pour 1 portion of the sauce into the pan and mix it through. Stir in half of the cooked sausage mince. Keep stirring the polenta until it is a thick consistency. It should start to bubble. The timing can vary, so you need to watch the mixture closely. Be careful not to undercook your polenta or it will be runny and not set properly.

5 To serve, spoon some sugo into individual bowls, sprinkle with Parmigiano, and layer the polenta on top. Add more sugo, a sprinkle of sausage mince and extra Parmigiano. Serve with the ribs and sausage on the side.

NONNA IGEA'S TIPS

- You might choose to use an instant polenta if it is hard to find fresh, but make sure you pay attention to the instructions, so it doesn't overcook and harden.
- The best way to test if your polenta is ready is to put a small portion on a plate with sugo and taste it. If it is still really runny, it needs to cook a little more so it becomes beautifully dense, but not hard.
- Nonna's polenta is best enjoyed hot, so don't wait for it to harden before eating, as the harder texture completely changes the experience.

SPAGHETTI ALLA NERANO
SPAGHETTI WITH ZUCCHINI AND PROVOLONE

This pasta dish may sound simple, but the original recipe has never been revealed. Deriving from Nerano, near the Amalfi Coast, it was first cooked up in a local family restaurant, where it is still proudly made today. While they have held tightly to their secrets, Vincenzo has masterfully paid homage to it and the creaminess is on-par with the original version (we think so anyway!). Thinly sliced pieces of zucchini fried until just crisp, lathered in cheese and twisted around strands of spaghetti make for a light, salty, satisfying dish. Just don't overcook the zucchini when you are too busy daydreaming about your next holiday! It may or may not have happened during the making of this book ... Oops!

SERVES 2–3
extra virgin olive oil (EVOO), qb
large bunch of basil, leaves picked
600g (21.1 oz) zucchini, sliced into thin, even discs
150g (5.5 oz) provolone dolce
1 tbsp rock salt
300g (10.6 oz) spaghetti pasta
1 garlic clove
3 tbsp finely grated Pecorino Romano or Parmigiano Reggiano

METHOD

1 Heat a generous amount of EVOO in a small saucepan over medium heat. Line a plate with paper towel. Place some of the basil leaves on top. Test the temperature of the oil by adding a small piece of zucchini – if it bubbles, the oil is ready. Fry the zucchini in batches, moving it around occasionally with a slotted spoon, for a few minutes or until the zucchini starts to turn crisp and is cooked through. Keep an eye on the oil temperature and adjust if needed. Once fried, transfer to the prepared plate to absorb excess oil and infuse with the basil.

2 While the zucchini is frying, grate the provolone and set aside.

3 Bring a large pot of water to a rolling boil, add rock salt, allow to dissolve and then cook your pasta according to the packet instructions.

4 Meanwhile, in a frying pan, heat a generous drizzle of EVOO over low heat. Smash the garlic clove and add to the pan to infuse the oil for 1–2 minutes, stirring occasionally. About 1–2 minutes before the pasta is ready, reserve a small portion of zucchini and basil for garnish. Add the remainder to the frying pan to warm it up.

5 Once the pasta is almost ready, reserve two-thirds of a mug of pasta water, then drain it. Remove the garlic clove from the frying pan and add the pasta to the pan, along with half the reserved pasta water. Toss with tongs to combine. Remove from heat, then stir in the cheese and some remaining basil leaves (whole or torn). Toss to create a creamy sauce. Add the remaining provolone and most of the remaining pasta water, mixing until creamy. If needed, add extra pasta water to prevent the cheese from sticking. Toss gently to avoid breaking the zucchini slices, but be quick.

6 The cheese can easily start to harden, so move fast and serve up individual portions using a set of tongs. Garnish each plate with reserved crispy zucchini, any remaining freshly torn basil, and a sprinkle of Pecorino or freshly ground pepper – or even both.

VINCENZO'S TIPS
- Take your time when cutting the zucchini or use a mandoline. Remember, the thinner you cut them, the quicker they will cook and the more likely they will break when you are mixing.
- Cook up a small test batch first of zucchini to check how tender/crispy you like it. It will only take a couple of minutes to cook through – and remember, you add it back into a hot pan where it will cook a little more at the end of the process.

SPAGHETTI AGLIO, OLIO E PEPERONCINO

While this might be one of the simplest recipes in this book, this dish is not without flavour, despite minimal ingredients. For us, it is synonymous with one of our most memorable moments with Vincenzo's papà, Paolo. It was his 60th birthday, and we had just enjoyed a big celebration at an idyllic villa not too far from Vincenzo's home town of Pescara. As the clock was ticking into the early hours and only a handful of friends and family were still around, Paolo headed into the kitchen for our 'spaghetti at midnight' feast and cooked up, you guessed it, Spaghetti aglio, olio e peperoncino.

It was like nothing we had ever eaten and we each devoured every last strand of pasta, even though we had enjoyed a big dinner! It begs the question too: is it about the dish, the recipe or the moment?

SERVES 3–4
1 tbsp rock salt
300g (10.6 oz) spaghetti pasta
100–120ml (3.4–4 fl oz) extra virgin olive oil (EVOO), plus extra for drizzling
2 garlic cloves, crushed
2 hot red chillies, finely chopped (optional)
bunch of flat-leaf (Italian) parsley, leaves and stems finely chopped
finely grated Pecorino Romano, and black pepper, to serve (optional)

METHOD

1 Bring a large pot of water to a rolling boil, add rock salt, and allow to dissolve. Add the pasta and cook it for 2 minutes less than in the packet instructions. When the pasta is almost ready, collect a mug of pasta water.

2 While the pasta cooks, heat a large frying pan over medium heat. As it starts to warm up, add the EVOO. Add the garlic and chilli and mix gently using a wooden spoon, before adding a pinch or two of chopped parsley. Mix again, leaving it to sizzle and glisten until the garlic starts to turn slightly golden.

3 Add half the reserved pasta water to the frying pan and let it simmer and bubble, mixing with the wooden spoon and even whisking slightly to create a thicker consistency.

4 Using tongs, transfer the pasta to the frying pan. Mix it thoroughly with the oil, keeping the pan over medium heat so the pasta finishes cooking. Add another splash of pasta water, along with a generous drizzle of EVOO and a pinch of parsley and chilli, if using. Use the tongs to combine, making sure every strand is dripping with the liquid gold you have created. Add a final drizzle of EVOO, one last splash of pasta water, and more parsley and chilli (if you're all about the heat) and toss.

5 Plate up, sprinkle with more parsley, chilli and, if you can't help yourself, another drizzle of EVOO. While it's not common practice, we also love this with a generous sprinkle of grated Pecorino and a good serve of ground black pepper.

VINCENZO'S TIPS
- Invest in a good-quality garlic crusher. Crushing garlic releases its essential oils and produces a more intense flavour than chopping does.
- Don't underestimate the creaminess you get from adding the pasta water. Take your time to thicken the mixture by almost whisking it before adding the pasta.
- Although I love this with Pecorino on top, you could try toasted breadcrumbs and freshly ground black pepper.

GNOCCHI ALLA SORRENTINA

When I first tried Gnocchi alla Sorrentina in Sorrento, I was hooked from the first bite. Since then, we've made it at home countless times, always with plenty of cheese. If you've never tried it, this dish is gnocchi smothered in a rich tomato sugo and baked with an abundance of mozzarella. If you're unsure how much cheese to add, go for more – you can't go wrong (the less is more rule doesn't apply to cheese in our home).

This dish is a classic from Sorrento, showcasing three of Campania's stars: juicy tomatoes, fragrant basil and creamy mozzarella. As the cheese melts into the sauce, it creates an irresistibly gooey texture, which is pure comfort food. Sensational, delicious and oh so cheesy.

SERVES 4
extra virgin olive oil (EVOO), qb
2 garlic cloves, crushed
700g (24.7 oz) bottle store-bought passata or use homemade (see recipe, page 74) or 2 × 400g (14.1 oz) canned whole peeled Italian tomatoes, blended in a blender for 10 seconds
salt and pepper
1 tbsp rock salt
400g (14.1 oz) ricotta or potato gnocchi (or use homemade, see recipes, pages 92, 95)
2 fresh fior di latte or buffalo mozzarella balls, cut into medium-sized cubes
Pecorino Romano or Parmigiano Reggiano, finely grated, qb
small bunch of basil

METHOD

1 Heat a large ovenproof skillet or deep frying pan over low heat. Add 3–4 tbsp EVOO and garlic. Once the garlic starts to bubble (about 20 seconds), stir in the passata or blended tomato. Season. Simmer, stirring occasionally, for 15 minutes. Remove from heat and set aside.

2 Preheat the oven grill (broiler) to 180°C (360°F).

3 Bring a large pot of water to a rolling boil, add rock salt, and allow to dissolve. Add gnocchi and stir gently. Once they float to the top, they're done – it should only take a few minutes.

4 While the gnocchi cook, check the sugo. If it's cool, reheat it gently over low heat.

5 Once the gnocchi are ready, drain and add straight to the sugo pan, then turn off the heat. Stir the gnocchi gently, coating well. Add half the mozzarella and mix. Sprinkle with 2 tbsp Pecorino or Parmigiano, followed by torn basil leaves, and mix again.

6 Scatter more mozzarella without mixing (save some to garnish), and more Pecorino, if desired. Place pan under grill for 5–10 minutes, keeping an eye on the cheese to make sure it doesn't turn brown/burn. Remove from oven and sit for 5 minutes to cool slightly.

7 Use a large serving spoon (not a deep one) to serve gnocchi into shallow bowls or flat plates, then sprinkle with a final touch of Pecorino and pepper, if you like. Scatter a few pieces of the remaining mozzarella on top of each serving – it's not traditional, but delicious. Otherwise, just snack on it before serving, unless you have a mozzarella-obsessed toddler like our Alessandro, who will rip it out of your hands once it's in sight.

VINCENZO'S TIPS
- All of your ingredients can be prepared ahead of time. If you are making fresh gnocchi, do this the day before and your dish will be ready in no time.
- No time to make gnocchi? Buy quality store-bought potato gnocchi and cook according to the packet instructions. They need to melt in your mouth like Nonna's!
- While the traditional recipe calls for fior di latte mozzarella, opting for buffalo mozzarella adds a new dimension. If you can find buffalo mozzarella, you will taste the difference.
- Cut the mozzarella into medium-sized cubes for even melting – too small and they brown too quickly; too large and they may not melt properly. Strain the mozzarella well to remove excess water.

SPAGHETTI AL LIMONE LEMON PASTA

Let this citrus recipe transport you to the sun-drenched shores of Sicily or the Amalfi Coast. Light, creamy and bursting with fragrant lemon flavour, it's a true celebration of simple, quality ingredients, and if you're keeping up, yes, this is a recurring theme.

The secret? Fresh, organic lemons. When they're in season, their vibrant aroma and natural sweetness make all the difference. But even if they're not, you can still create something beautiful. Just promise one thing: skip the bottled lemon juice. Only fresh juice and fragrant zest will give you that bright, authentic taste. And no cream is needed here. Just the perfect balance of zest and juice to let the lemons shine (and to keep Vincenzo's heart intact!). The result is irresistibly smooth and luscious. Vincenzo often whips this up when guests drop by unexpectedly, and it never lasts long. It's a guaranteed crowd-pleaser – kids included!

SERVES 2
1 tbsp rock salt
200g (7 oz) spaghetti pasta
3 lemons, plus 1 extra for extra zest and garnish
80ml (2.7 fl oz) extra virgin olive oil (EVOO)
small bunch of mint or basil
small bowl of finely grated Pecorino Romano

METHOD

1 Bring a large pot of water to a rolling boil, add rock salt, and allow to dissolve. Add the pasta and cook it for 2 minutes less than in the packet instructions.

2 While the pasta cooks, zest lemons onto a plate. Zest extra for a richer lemon flavour. Cut 2 lemons in half and squeeze the juice into a glass or bowl. Reserve the lemon halves. Pour the EVOO into a large frying pan over medium–high heat. Add three-quarters of the lemon zest and half the juice, then tear a handful of mint or basil leaves and add them in. Place the reserved lemon halves in the pan, flat side down, for extra flavour.

3 Once the pasta is ready, drain it, reserving a mug of pasta water. Transfer the pasta to the frying pan with the lemon mixture. Pour in just over half the reserved pasta water and turn the heat to high. For the first minute, constantly stir while the pasta water evaporates. Remove the lemon halves and cook the pasta for another 30 seconds. Add almost all remaining zest (reserving some for garnish) and more mint leaves plus the rest of the lemon juice and keep mixing for another minute, or until all the water has evaporated.

4 Remove the pan from heat and add the Pecorino. Toss quickly to coat the strands of pasta while it's off the stove or it will coagulate and become stringy. Use tongs to transfer generous portions of pasta to plates. Scoop up any leftover sauce and drizzle it over each portion. Top with reserved lemon zest and mint leaves.

VINCENZO'S TIPS

- This pasta needs to be cooked a little less than the packet suggests because the last few minutes of the cooking time will be done in the frying pan.
- If scaling this for an unexpected crowd, use 1 medium lemon per serving, plus 1 extra for extra zest and garnish.
- I know, I know, I've swayed from tradition here – but you must admit, the pairing of lemon and mint is undoubtedly perfect, right? You be the judge! If you want a more authentic flavour, swap out the mint for basil.
- When adding the grated Pecorino, add it gradually while stirring continuously to avoid clumping and to ensure the sauce remains smooth. If the sauce becomes too thick, thin it out with some reserved pasta water.

PIZZA E PANE

PIZZA E PANE

This chapter celebrates dough in all its glorious forms. Whether blistered into the perfect pizza crust or baked into a rustic loaf that cracks as you tear it open, few things are more comforting than that first bite. Close your eyes and imagine it: a crisp-yet-pillowy pizza base beneath your favourite toppings, or warm bread dipped into golden extra virgin olive oil. We have included select recipes here, to kickstart and refine your journey to mastering dough at home, and they will no doubt ignite a desire for more carb-filled joy and flour-dusted countertops in your life.

Vincenzo's love for traditional pizza was sealed after a memorable trip to Italy's capital of pizza, Naples, where local friends led him on an adventure filled with a whirlwind of flavours. They fed him more pizza in a few short days than he ever thought possible! As he wandered the vibrant streets, each slice deepened his admiration for the artistry, simplicity and passion baked into every crust. He left the city not only full, but also determined to respect and master the time-honoured methods that make Neapolitan pizza so iconic.

He didn't stop at pizza, but was inspired to create dough recipes for both pizza and bread that could be mastered by anyone – no wood-fired oven or Italian baking pedigree required. Through experimentation, he perfected a no-knead bread that became a viral sensation, proving that incredible, crusty loaves can be made right at home. And like pizza, bread is woven deeply into the fabric of Italian life, so essential that it's rarely missing from the table. (In fact, we often hide it from our two sons, who will devour it before anything else the moment it appears!)

PIZZA NAPOLETANA AUTHENTIC NEAPOLITAN PIZZA

Nothing gets Vincenzo dancing in the kitchen more than when he is recreating this incomparable Neapolitan pizza dough recipe. It came from the legendary Italo-Australian pizza maestro Johnny Di Francesco, and if you follow our channel, it barely needs an introduction. The video recipe these two filmed together has amassed millions of views, and for good reason: it comes with all the tips and tricks to perfecting the dough and will rival even your favourite pizzeri.

Imagine the artistry of a dough made with just four simple ingredients – flour, water, salt and yeast – coming together to create a soft, airy crust with that iconic *cornicione* (the golden, raised edge blistered by the intense heat of a wood-fired oven). Each bite takes you to the heart of Naples, with a smoky char that's simply irresistible.

To experience authentic Neapolitan pizza is to partake in a ritual, a journey to the streets of Naples. Can't get to Naples? Get into the recipe below. Vincenzo swears by it.

MAKES 6 PIZZAS
600ml (20.3 fl oz) cold tap water
5 tsp (30g/1 oz) table (fine) salt
1kg (35.3 oz) pizza or tipo '00' flour, plus extra for dusting
2g (0.1 oz) fresh yeast or ½ tsp instant dry yeast

SPECIAL EQUIPMENT
cook's thermometer
1 large airtight container with a lid
wood-fired oven
pizza peel

METHOD

1 Pour the water into a large bowl and add the salt. Mix well using one hand to help dissolve. Add 100g (3.5 oz) flour and mix until the flour is incorporated.

2 Dissolve the yeast into the mixture (breaking up with your fingers if fresh) and mix by hand. Gradually add the remaining flour, a little at a time, mixing as you go. Hold the bowl with one hand and turn it while scraping down any flour from the side with your other hand to ensure everything combines smoothly.

3 Once the dough starts to come together, flip it out onto a bench and knead it with both hands to absorb all the remaining flour. Keep kneading until it comes together, has a smooth consistency and when you press down on the dough ball with one finger, it bounces back. Aim for an internal temperature of 23–26°C (73–79°F).

4 Set aside the dough on a flat surface and cover with a damp tea towel so it doesn't dry out. Leave it for 2 hours to rest.

5 Make the pizza balls by first cutting the dough into 6 pieces, weighing 250g (8.8 oz) each. Roll each portion in a circular motion, using the palm of your hand, over and over again in one spot, until it is round with smooth surfaces. Transfer the dough balls to an airtight container and leave in an ambient environment with a temperature of 16–18°C (61–64°F) for 24 hours.

Continued on next page >

PIZZA NAPOLETANA AUTHENTIC NEAPOLITAN PIZZA (CONT'D)

6 When you are ready to make your pizza, preheat the oven to 400°C (750°F).

7 Your dough balls should have risen and be ready to use. Sprinkle extra flour on the bench and place a dough ball on top. Starting an inch from the edge closest to you, press the dough down using your fingers until you're 2–3cm (1 inch) from the top edge. Then stop, turn it over and repeat until you have a small round base with a cornicione (crust).

8 Stretch the base by picking up the dough and gently pulling it over one forearm, then flipping it onto the bench. Repeat before shaping it into a circle by moving it around on top of the floured bench, then rest it on the bench. Move on to steps 9 and 10 before shaping the next base.

9 Add your favourite toppings, then carefully slide the dough onto the pizza peel. Shape it to keep it round, but don't touch it too much. Put the peel inside the oven, then place it down near the back and quickly, with a flick of the wrist, remove the peel, leaving the pizza in the oven. Don't move back and forth or scrape the peel across the base of the oven as you will just move ash around.

10 When you see one side of the pizza start to turn golden (or after 30 seconds), leave it for another 5 seconds, then slide the peel under the pizza from one side in just one motion, pull it out, turn it just halfway round, then put it back in. This way there is no residue on the pizza base. Cook for 30 seconds, then turn one more time, and once ready, lift it slightly, to toast the top, for no more than 3 seconds, turning it slightly. Your pizza should cook for no more than 90 seconds in total. The base should be spotty and golden, but not charred, and the cornicione should bounce back once pressed gently. Slice and serve hot.

JOHNNY'S TIPS
- To make a good Neapolitan pizza, aim to source a flour that includes 11–13g (0.4 oz) protein, such as pizza flour or tipo '00' flour.
- When adding yeast to the mixture, never contaminate the salt with the yeast. By mixing the yeast in when there's about 10 per cent of the total flour in the salt-water mixture, you will evenly distribute it throughout the dough without it coming into direct contact with the salt.
- If you want to use a stand mixer, start by mixing the water, salt and 10 per cent of the flour until combined. Dissolve the yeast separately, add it to the wet mixture, then gradually add the remaining flour while mixing. Once it is combined, flip the dough onto a floured bench and start the kneading process.
- For further tips, see the Pizza Margherita recipe, page 172.

FOCACCIA GENOVESE

This iconic bread from Genoa in northwestern Italy is a culinary masterpiece. With its golden colour, delicate air pockets and perfectly not-too-thick crumb, it has the ideal balance of crispy edges and a soft divine centre. Although the recipe itself is a classic, Vincenzo has added a touch of his own flair, topping it with cherry tomatoes that balance sweetness, acidity and the warmth of the crust, creating a bite that reads like a little poem on the palate. This focaccia can be devoured at any time of day, for any craving. Legend has it that locals in Genoa even love it dipped in their cappuccinos – though you might want to skip the cherry tomatoes if you're trying it that way!

SERVES 4–8

3 tbsp extra virgin olive oil (EVOO), plus extra for drizzling
200ml (6.7 fl oz) cold tap water
350g (12.3 oz) plain (all-purpose) flour, plus extra for dusting
7g (0.2 oz) sachet instant dried yeast
1 tsp honey
2 tsp (10g/0.3 oz) table (fine) salt
pinch of sea salt
handful of cherry tomatoes, halved
a few rosemary leaves, finely chopped, or a sprinkle of dried oregano

SPECIAL EQUIPMENT

stand mixer with dough hook attachment (can also be made by hand)
38 × 27 × 3cm (15 × 10.6 × 1.9 inch) or a round 28 x 5cm (11 x 2 inch) non-stick baking tray

METHOD

1 Place the EVOO in the bowl of a stand mixer and use paper towel or a pastry brush to coat the bowl evenly. Add the water and 2 heaped tbsp flour. Pour in the yeast and mix well with a spoon. Add the honey, half the remaining flour and, using a stand mixer and the hook attachment, start mixing on low speed. Once you see the ingredients coming together, increase to medium for 5 minutes, or until well combined. Next, add the table (fine) salt and the rest of the flour and mix on high speed for 15 minutes or until a dough has formed with a thick, moist consistency. You can also do this by hand; it will just take a little longer to come together.

2 Dust a flat surface with extra flour, then place the dough on top. Add some flour to your hands, then fold the dough over a couple of times, mixing in the flour on the board and from your hands until it forms a large ball. Cover the dough with a clean tea towel and let it rest for 15 minutes. Meanwhile, use your pastry brush to lather a baking tray with a generous amount of extra EVOO.

3 After 15 minutes, remove the towel and gently lift the dough, as it may stick. Fold it over, stretch slightly and press down with your fingertips, poking it all over. Fold it again to lengthen it, pressing down a few times. Place it in the centre of the prepared tray, coat with EVOO, cover with a towel and let it rest for 1 more hour.

4 Remove the towel – your dough should be well risen. Use your fingertips to spread it out, fully covering the tray base. Sprinkle a pinch of sea salt over the top of the dough, then let it rest once again, covered, for 1–2 hours.

5 Remove the towel. Combine a small amount of water with a drizzle of EVOO and spread it over the dough with a pastry brush. Press down all over the dough using your fingertips. Place the tomato halves, seed side up, on the focaccia and sprinkle with rosemary, then allow to rest, uncovered, for 1 more hour.

6 Preheat the oven to 220°C (430°F). Bake for 15–20 minutes, or until it starts to turn golden. Remove from the tray and place on a wire rack to rest before serving.

VINCENZO'S TIPS
- Be generous when pouring EVOO over the dough. This not only helps to form a soft crust but also keeps the bread moist.
- If not baking immediately, refrigerate the dough for up to 24 hours, but remove it 2 hours before baking to reach room temperature.

NO-KNEAD ARTISAN BREAD

Making bread is no easy feat ... unless you follow this recipe to create the crustiest loaf, with no kneading required. When Vincenzo started recipe testing this bread, we were left in awe every time at how delicious it turned out. It's essentially a no-fail recipe that will leave you feeling like a baking pro. It's that good.

This recipe bakes up the most golden, crunchy crust enveloping a soft, pillowy interior. Serving up warm slices with extra virgin olive oil is enough to get your tastebuds watering, or try smothering slices with lashings of ricotta and a generous drizzle of honey.

There isn't a lot to think about here. If you love bread and want to indulge in a homemade version, get to know this four-ingredient recipe. It will likely be on rotation in your oven pretty quickly.

MAKES 1 LOAF
400g (14 oz) plain (all-purpose) flour or tipo '00' flour, plus extra for dusting
300ml (10 fl oz) lukewarm water
$1/2$ tsp instant dry yeast
1 tbsp table (fine) salt

SPECIAL EQUIPMENT
25–28cm (10–11 inch) diameter Dutch oven or cast iron deep round casserole or an ovenproof stainless steel pot

METHOD

1 Place a handful of flour in a large bowl along with the lukewarm water. Mix using a spatula or fork, then add the yeast and mix until it dissolves. Add another handful of flour and continue to mix, then add the salt. Mix until the salt has disappeared, then add the remaining flour and mix again. The dough should be wet and sticky. Cover the bowl tightly with plastic wrap and leave to rest for 6 hours at room temperature. Then rest in the fridge for 12 hours.

2 After it's rested, remove from the fridge, then place the dough on a chopping board or the kitchen bench. Dust the top of the dough with some extra flour, then turn it over and add some to the bottom, rubbing it in. Stretch the dough out, fold it over about a quarter of the way, then again three more times until you have folded it completely. Turn it around and repeat the process, adding flour as you go.

3 Get a clean bowl, place a sheet of baking (parchment) paper inside it, dust it with extra flour and put the dough inside, with one more sprinkle of flour on top. Fold the paper over so the dough is covered and leave it to rest for 2 hours at room temperature.

4 Halfway through the resting process, preheat the oven to 250°C (480°F) and place a Dutch oven or cast-iron deep round casserole inside, empty, with the lid on, so it warms up for 1 hour.

5 After the dough has rested, decrease the oven to 230°C (445°F). Carefully remove the Dutch oven and place your dough inside. Make two light slits on the surface, creating a cross. Put the lid on the Dutch oven and place it back in the oven for 30 minutes. Then remove the lid and continue to bake for another 15–20 minutes, or until golden and crispy. Remove the bread from the oven and the Dutch oven, and put it on a rack to cool for at least 10 minutes, then devour!

VINCENZO'S TIPS
- This dough will initially be sticky but will shape up later. Don't be tempted to add more flour.
- Take your time! This no-knead recipe works because of the rising time, so make careful note. If you leave it for a little longer it will still turn out beautifully, just don't let it rest for less.
- The dutch oven must be preheated – don't miss this. When you set the room-temperature dough inside, the outside layer cooks quickly, resulting in the perfect crust.
- Wait for the bread to cool slightly before slicing, otherwise it can tear or result in a gummy interior.

PIZZA MARGHERITA

Enter the world of Vincenzo's all-time favourite pizza: the Margherita. History tells us it was developed for Queen Margherita of Savoy in 1889, who declared it the best pizza she had ever eaten. Over a century later, Vincenzo feels much the same. Topped simply with tomatoes, mozzarella and basil, it also represents the colours of the Italian flag, so is quite the patriotic symbol.

For Vincenzo, this recipe, passed on from award-winning pizzaiolo Lucio de Falco, is an important one. If you can master a Margherita pizza, it is like passing the test to achieve pizza greatness, and after that it might just seem like anything is possible. Using the finest ingredients, a few simple steps and a dash of technique, you'll create a pizza that's as close to the one served on the streets of Naples as you can get, a true Italian classic that never goes out of style.

MAKES 1 PIZZA
1 × dough ball (see recipe, page 164)
⅓ cup (80ml/2.7 fl oz) Tomato sauce for pizza (see recipe, page 73)
100g (3.5 oz) fresh fior di latte or buffalo mozzarella, drained and cut into 1cm (0.4 inch) thick pieces
handful of finely grated Pecorino Romano
handful of basil leaves
extra virgin olive oil (EVOO), for drizzling

SPECIAL EQUIPMENT
pizza oven: electric, gas or wood-fired (you can also use a conventional oven with a pizza stone or baking tray; it will still be a Margherita, just not Neapolitan)
pizza peel

METHOD

1 Preheat a pizza oven to 400°C (750°F). If using a conventional oven, see tip below.

2 Roll out the dough ball into a pizza base as per the instructions on page 167.

3 Using the back of a serving spoon, spread the sauce evenly over the pizza base, avoiding the cornicione area. Top with a generous amount of fior di latte or mozzarella strips and a sprinkle of Pecorino. Add a few basil leaves before a drizzle of EVOO.

4 Carefully place the pizza on a pizza peel and slide it into the oven. The pizza should be cooked for a maximum of 90 seconds, turning 180° halfway through – and be sure to check the bottom in between to ensure it does not burn. Serve it hot.

LUCIO'S TIPS
- If using a wood-fired oven, when turning the pizza, briefly remove it from the oven using the pizza peel to ensure even cooking, safely rotating without burning yourself or disrupting the toppings.
- If you don't have a pizza oven, preheat a conventional oven and pizza stone or baking tray to 250°C (480°F). Top the rolled-out dough with tomato sauce and par-bake on a pizza stone (or lined baking tray) for 3–5 minutes. Remove from the oven, add the cheese, basil and EVOO and cook for another 5 minutes, or until the crust is golden and the cheese is melted and bubbly.
- For an authentic Pizza Margherita, it's essential to use high-quality ingredients, such as fresh mozzarella. Its moisture helps prevent burning during the baking process. I really dislike shredded cheese, so if you usually use this but can source quality mozzarella instead, don't hesitate – you will never look back.
- You can also add the basil after the tomato sauce and cover it with the cheese so it doesn't burn or wilt in the oven.

NO-KNEAD CIABATTA BREAD LOAVES

Instead of heading to the bakery and buying bread rolls made with unknown ingredients, why not make your own with minimal effort? Our eldest son, Sebastian, has loved bread since he started solids, and Vincenzo shares this love, which led him on a mission to create the perfect recipe for the whole family. Now, we are hooked on making fresh panini at least twice a week.

In Italian cuisine, bread isn't just a side; it's a staple that accompanies every meal. A fresh loaf symbolises warmth, togetherness and the joy of sharing good food. Whether mopping up a rich pasta sauce, pairing with minestrone soup or enjoying it with extra virgin olive oil, bread is sacred.

These ciabatta loaves freeze well and require no kneading. With this recipe, you'll create delicious, airy, crusty loaves that make your kitchen smell like an Italian bakery – why are you even hesitating?!

MAKES 4–6 LOAVES (DEPENDING ON SIZE)
400g (14 oz) plain (all-purpose) flour or tipo '00' flour, plus extra for dusting
300ml (10 fl oz) room temperature water
12g (0.4 oz) fresh yeast or 1 tsp instant dry yeast
2 tbsp extra virgin olive oil (EVOO), plus extra for drizzling
1 tsp white (granulated) sugar
1 tbsp table (fine) salt

METHOD

1 Place a handful of flour in a large bowl along with the lukewarm water. Mix using a spatula or fork, then add the yeast (breaking up with your fingers if fresh) and mix until it dissolves. Add the EVOO, then the sugar and salt, and mix until incorporated. Slowly add the remaining flour, just 10–20 per cent at a time, mixing it as you go to make sure the flour is fully absorbed into the wet mixture. Cover the bowl with plastic wrap and place in the oven (turned off) for 2 hours to rest or until it's sticky and almost double in size, although the flavours will continue to develop for up to 24 hours if you're patient!

2 Remove the bowl from the oven, dust a board with a generous sprinkle of extra flour, then place the dough on the board.

3 Preheat the oven to 230°C (445°F). Fill a medium cake pan with water and place it in the bottom of the oven. This helps keep the bread from drying out.

4 Drizzle a generous amount of EVOO on top of the dough, spreading it all over, before using the spatula to fold in each side of the bread, one section at a time (some of the flour will now be stuck to the dough). Sprinkle with extra flour, spreading it all over.

5 Line a tray with baking (parchment) paper. Cut the dough into 4–6 roughly even portions using a sharp knife, or a dough cutter, and gently lift each one (with a hand on either end) and place it on the prepared tray.

6 Place the tray in the oven and bake for 20 minutes before removing the cake pan of water and baking the loaves for an additional 5 minutes. Remove from the oven and rest on a wire rack for 5–7 minutes, then enjoy.

VINCENZO'S TIPS
- Mix the ingredients thoroughly. Even though you don't need to knead the dough, you still need to mix the ingredients well to ensure they are evenly distributed. Use a sturdy wooden spoon or spatula to mix until the dough is smooth and elastic.
- To easily remove the dough from the bowl, wet the tip of a spatula or your hands with warm water.
- You can use a knife to separate portions of dough, but a dough scraper is best to use, if you have one.
- Wrap any leftover loaves tightly in plastic wrap and freeze for up to 3 months. To keep crisp, thaw at room temperature, then reheat in a 180°C (360°F) oven for 5–10 minutes, or until warmed and crispy.

PIZZE FRITTE DELLA NONNA IGEA   FRIED PIZZA, ABRUZZO STYLE

Nonna Igea's fried pizza recipe is the stuff of neighbourhood legend – literally, her neighbours have requested she make a batch for their functions for years! Picture this: a delightful hybrid of bread, pizza and savoury doughnut – all parts delicious. Biting into one of these freshly fried wonders is like sinking into a soft, airy and downright dreamy cloud. While Nonna typically serves them plain, feel free to get creative by shaping them into calzone, or keeping them round and topping with cheese and deli meats.

SERVES 8

2 cups (500ml/16.9 fl oz) full cream milk
50g (1.7 oz) salted butter
100ml (3.4 fl oz) lukewarm water
25g (0.9 oz) fresh yeast or 14g (0.2 oz) dry yeast
1 egg, beaten
1kg (35 oz) plain (all-purpose) flour, plus extra for dusting
1 tsp white (granulated) sugar
2 tbsp table (fine) salt
sunflower oil, for deep-frying

METHOD

1 In a large saucepan, heat the milk just enough to warm it up – don't bring to the boil. Add the butter, allow it to melt, then mix to combine. Remove from the heat and set aside.

2 Pour the lukewarm water into a glass, then add the yeast. Mix using your fingers until it dissolves. In a large bowl, combine the egg and flour using a fork, then pour in the yeast mixture and mix again.

3 Add the sugar and salt and mix through along with the milk mixture, continuing to combine with a fork. Then start to mix with your hands, scraping the side of the bowl and mixing in any remaining flour. Continue until all ingredients are combined and a soft dough forms.

4 Transfer ransfer the dough to a flat surface dusted with extra flour. Using the base of your palm, knead the dough by rolling it back and forth a few times, then fold it in half and turn it over. Knead for up to 5 minutes and your dough should be smooth and ready.

5 Dust the base of a clean large bowl with flour and place the dough in the bowl. Cover with a clean tea towel or plastic wrap and rest at room temperature for 3 hours or until doubled in size.

6 Remove the dough from the bowl and knead it again for just a few minutes. Slice the dough into portions about 2.5cm (1 inch) thick, then cut each portion into about 3–4 small pieces before rolling each one into a small ball, about the size of a golf ball.

7 Lightly flour your surface, then use a rolling pin to roll out each ball into a thin circle resembling a mini pizza. Roll out until they are about 5mm ($1/4$ inch) thick and 10–15cm (4–6 inches) in diameter (they will get bigger when you fry them). Cut a slit in the middle of each one – this will help them cook through. Repeat with the remaining dough and leave them to rest on a large, flat surface.

8 Heat a generous amount of oil in a frying pan until it reaches 180°C (360°F) or small bubbles appear around the handle of a wooden spoon. Once the oil is hot, lay the dough rounds in, a few at a time, being careful not to overcrowd the pan. Cook batches of the same number each time so you get used to the length of time they need. They cook fast and puff right up to the surface. Using a fork, frequently flip the dough until each one becomes golden brown on both sides. Remove from the oil using a slotted spoon and place on a plate lined with paper towel to cool.

NONNA IGEA'S TIPS

- The best way to knead the dough is by hand. (You can use a stand mixer with a dough hook, but Nonna wouldn't dream of it.)
- To make mini calzone, start with larger circles at step 7, put your filling and an easy-melting cheese into the centre of the dough, then fold over like a raviolo. Crease the edges with a fork and don't make a slit in them.
- If it's your first time, fry one at a time to gauge cooking time and avoid burning. To prevent any hot oil splashes, I lay the dough away from me when putting it into the pan.

NO-KNEAD NEAPOLITAN PIZZA DOUGH

Love making pizza, but not kneading dough? This one is for you! Traditional Neapolitan pizza dough typically needs lots of kneading, so Vincenzo teamed up with Naples pizza masters Gigio Attanasio, Vincenzo Viscusi and Antonio Pascarella, on a mission to craft a dry-yeast no-knead version, and it's an absolute game changer. While the dough rests and rises, you'll have time to prep your ingredients and set the scene for pizza night. With this simple method, just follow the measurements precisely and you'll get a light, airy crust and perfectly textured base without much effort.

MAKES 6 PIZZAS
1kg (35 oz) pizza or tipo '00' flour
¼ tsp (1g/0.1 oz) instant dry yeast
20g (0.7 oz) salt
700ml (24 fl oz) water
fine semolina flour or pizza or tipo '00' flour, for stretching dough
extra virgin olive oil (EVOO), for coating

SPECIAL EQUIPMENT
6 individual airtight containers or 1 large airtight container
pizza oven: electric, gas or wood-fired (you can also use a conventional oven with a pizza stone or baking tray)
pizza peel

METHOD

1 In a large bowl, mix the pizza or tipo '00' flour, yeast and salt by hand. Add the water and use a wooden spoon to blend, scooping in the flour, until combined – it will be a rough dough, not smooth. At this point, the dough won't have much structure. Cover the bowl with a plate or plastic wrap and leave it in the fridge for 10–16 hours.

2 Once rested, the dough should be pliable and workable. Tip the dough onto a clean benchtop and stretch into a rectangle. Fold the top third down to the centre, then fold the bottom third up over it, like folding a letter. Repeat this letter fold once more. Shape into a ball by folding it in half, then rolling gently until round. Once smooth, cover it with an upside-down bowl and let it rest for 15–20 minutes.

3 Divide the dough into 6 portions of 250g (8.8 oz) each. After weighing, reshape each piece into a ball by folding and closing it, then roll slightly. Add a few drops of EVOO to 6 airtight containers (or 1 large) and rub to coat the sides. Place the dough balls inside, cover with the lid and rest at 18–21°C (64–70°F) for 4 hours.

4 Preheat the pizza oven to 400°C (750°F).

5 Spread a small handful of semolina or pizza or tipo '00' flour over the bench. Sprinkle a portion of flour around the edge of one dough ball while still in the container. If stored individually, flip one of the containers upside down to release the dough onto the flour pile.

6 Flip the dough twice, starting to shape as you go. Gently press down with your fingers, starting at the bottom and slowly working outward, leaving a rim around the edge for the crust. Flip, then repeat. You should end up with a traditional shape (thin middle with thicker crust).

7 To remove excess flour, pick up the dough and let it hang slightly off your hands to allow the flour to fall. Quickly add your sauce and toppings to prevent sticking. Carefully slide the pizza onto the peel, then into the oven. Bake for 60–90 seconds, rotating halfway. Repeat steps 5 to 7 for the remaining dough balls.

GIGIO, VINCENZO AND ANTONIO'S TIPS

- For leftover dough portions, store in the fridge for up to 3 days. For longer storage, wrap each dough ball in plastic wrap and freeze for up to 2 months.
- If you don't have a pizza oven, use an ovenproof frying pan and the oven grill (broiler). Preheat the grill to the second-highest setting and position the rack at the top. Heat a pan on the stove until it just starts smoking. Add the dough and wait for bubbles. Quickly add your toppings, and once the grill is red hot, transfer the pan to the oven for 100–120 seconds. For a charred 'leopard' crust, move the pan closer to the grill for the last 10 seconds.

SECONDI

SECONDI

Choosing the recipes for this chapter was no easy feat. Italy is often thought of as the land of pasta and pizza, but step beyond the primo and you'll find a treasure trove of main dishes, each with its own story and flavour. We've handpicked a selection that includes some of our beloved family favourites, alongside well-known classics like Saltimbocca and Chicken Cacciatore, in the hope they inspire your meals as much as they have ours.

Mains are richer and heartier, and often feature a protein at the centre of the plate. They're the dishes that shine at a Sunday lunch following a plate of pasta, or stand proudly on their own for a weekday dinner, sometimes lavish but always with simple ingredients. In Italy, there's no holding back: a main dish is about generosity, flavour and bringing everyone together.

Take Nonna's comforting Crepes in brodo, for instance. These delicate crepes, floating in a golden broth, are so exquisite they almost defy description. They're the kind of dish that warms your soul and brings a sense of home with every bite. There's my mamma Maria's Braciole alla Calabrese, a recipe that's practically a member of the family itself. Growing up, she often made these tender, flavour-packed meat rolls when we had guests over, setting the scene for long, joyful meals filled with laughter. And we can't forget Vincenzo's mamma, Graziella, who has perfected the art of Eggplant parmigiana. Her version is so divine she has been hands-down crowned a maestra.

Almost every recipe here holds a piece of our family history. We hope you'll feel inspired to recreate these dishes and share them with the people you cherish. They're designed to be savoured, to spark conversation and to turn even the simplest gathering into a lasting memory – one that inspires you to share stories, revisit traditions and create experiences that live on in your kitchen and beyond.

SALTIMBOCCA VEAL CUTLETS WITH PROSCIUTTO AND SAGE

Veal saltimbocca is one of those dishes that's all about big flavour, with almost no effort. It hails from Rome and its name translates as 'jump in the mouth', and once you take a bite, you'll understand why. It's a simple yet bold combination of tender veal, fresh sage and prosciutto. This is the kind of dish that's perfect when you need something that tastes like it took hours but can actually be done in no time. If you've ever ordered veal saltimbocca at a restaurant and wondered how it's made, prepare to be surprised. There are no complicated steps, just great ingredients and a little know-how. Pair with roasted potatoes and a side of Vincenzo's Grilled zucchini (see recipe, page 46).

SERVES 2
4 veal fillets, thinly sliced
4 thin slices Italian prosciutto crudo
small bunch of sage
bowl of plain (all-purpose) flour, for coating
1 tbsp extra virgin olive oil (EVOO)
50g (1.7 oz) butter
salt and pepper
½ glass white wine

SPECIAL EQUIPMENT
meat mallet
toothpicks

METHOD

1 Place the veal slices between sheets of baking (parchment) paper on a chopping board and flatten them gently with the flat side of a meat mallet for quick, even cooking.

2 Lay a veal slice on a plate, top it with a prosciutto slice to fit snugly, and place a sage leaf in the centre. Secure everything with a toothpick and repeat with the remaining veal and prosciutto, and more sage.

3 Lightly coat both sides of each veal slice with flour, shaking off any excess – this simple step ensures a silky, creamy sauce. Heat a large frying pan over medium–low heat, adding the EVOO and butter. Toss in a few sage leaves to infuse the butter with a fragrant, herby aroma.

4 Add the veal slices to the pan while the butter is still melting and cook for a couple of minutes until golden, then season with a pinch of salt and plenty of pepper.

5 Flip over each slice so the prosciutto side sizzles in the buttery goodness. Pour in the white wine and let it simmer until the alcohol evaporates. If it is sizzling too much, lower the heat slightly.

6 When the sauce thickens enough to coat the veal beautifully, it's ready to serve. Plate up each portion and scoop up some more sauce to add on top. Don't forget to remove the toothpicks before eating!

VINCENZO'S TIPS
- Ask your butcher for thin veal slices – trust me, they can even tenderise them for you. Thin cuts are crucial, so the veal cooks quickly and evenly, just like it should.
- Low and slow, that's the secret. Keep the heat on medium–low so the veal stays tender, juicy and packed with all those delicious flavours.
- Keep the veal moving in the pan with tongs or a fork. You don't want that butter to scorch – it'll turn your dish from fantastic to bitter, and we're here for flavour, not regret!

TRIPPA ALLA ROMANA ROMAN TRIPE

Truth be told, tripe isn't for everyone. I'm not the biggest fan, myself, but Vincenzo? He's obsessed, and so is practically everyone in his family. So, how could we not share it? The real magic of this recipe comes from the addition of pancetta or guanciale, which adds a delicious saltiness and depth of flavour. In Vincenzo's words, it 'takes the dish to the next level!'

Traditionally enjoyed in southern Italy, particularly in the regions of Campania and Calabria, tripe is often cooked in a rich sugo, slowly simmering to bring out its tenderness and absorb all those deep, savoury notes. This hearty dish was first crafted by Vincenzo's Nonna Gabriella (his papà's mamma), so when Vincenzo's parents met, mastering this family classic quickly became a top priority for his mamma, Graziella. And let's just say, she didn't just learn it – she conquered it. Graziella now proudly makes the best tripe in the family, and even Nonna Gabriella would raise her fork in approval!

SERVES 4

- 1kg (35.3 oz) honeycomb tripe, cleaned
- 2 carrots, 1 cut in half, 1 diced
- 1 brown onion, ½ left whole, ½ diced
- 2 celery stalks, 1 cut in half, 1 finely diced, leaves retained
- two pinches dried oregano
- 6 bay leaves
- ⅓ cup (80ml/2.7 fl oz) extra virgin olive oil (EVOO)
- 200g (7 oz) pancetta or guanciale, diced into cubes
- 1 glass white wine
- table (fine) salt
- 800g (14.1 oz) canned finely chopped Italian tomatoes
- pepper
- fresh chilli or dried chilli flakes (optional)
- crusty bread, to serve (try our No-knead artisan bread, see recipe, page 171)

METHOD

1 Add the whole tripe to a saucepan of water along with the halved pieces of carrot, onion and celery, a pinch of oregano and 3 bay leaves. Bring to the boil and cook for 10 minutes, then strain and set aside the tripe, discarding the liquid and other solids.

2 In another saucepan, warm the EVOO over medium heat. Add the diced carrot, onion and celery and cook until softened. Stir in the pancetta or guanciale and cook, moving it around occasionally, for a few minutes, or until browned and the fat has rendered. While this is cooking, cut the tripe into strips.

3 Add the tripe strips to the pan and stir to coat. Pour in the wine, sprinkle with salt and simmer for about 20 minutes, or until the wine has evaporated.

4 Stir in the tomatoes, then add the remaining 3 bay leaves, a glass of water, a pinch of oregano, pepper and the retained celery leaves. Mix everything together and cook over low heat for 30–35 minutes. For an extra kick, add fresh chilli now or sprinkle dried chilli flakes on top when serving.

5 Serve in bowls alongside crusty bread, and don't leave a single drop behind.

MAMMA GRAZIELLA'S TIPS

- Tripe is a tough cut of meat, so you have to cook it slowly over low heat in step 4, until it's nice and tender – don't rush it and don't take shortcuts! You'll know when it's ready – just give it time.
- Tripe can be a bit strong in flavour if it's not cleaned right, so make sure you give it a good boil with a generous pinch of oregano and plenty of fresh sage. Thyme, bay leaves, rosemary and fresh oregano would also work – just use what you have!

MELANZANE ALLA PARMIGIANA EGGPLANT PARMIGIANA

This is one of those recipes that Vincenzo and I share a common love for. Picture this: tender layers of perfectly fried eggplant, rich homemade tomato sugo, oozing melted cheese – all baked to golden perfection. While it might seem like a bit of work, once you take that first bite, you'll have zero regrets for the time spent frying and layering. The magic isn't just in the ingredients, it's in the process, and Vincenzo's mamma, Graziella, has passed on her recipe to us. It's deeply satisfying to make – almost meditative in the way the flavours develop and meld together. And the way that cheesy top creates a golden, bubbly crust? Pure heaven.

SERVES 6

2kg (70.5 oz) medium eggplants (aubergines)
table (fine) salt
plain (all-purpose) flour, for coating
sunflower oil, for deep-frying
1 batch Tomato and basil sugo (see recipe, page 60)
handful of basil leaves
Pecorino Romano, finely grated, qb
500g (17.6 oz) fresh mozzarella, drained and torn or cut into small pieces

SPECIAL EQUIPMENT

9 × 30cm (3.5 × 11.8 inch) glass baking dish (you could also use a 24cm (10 inch) round baking dish)

METHOD

1 Trim the top and bottom of each eggplant, then slice lengthways into 1cm (½ inch) thick pieces. Layer half the slices in a colander and sprinkle generously with salt. Repeat with the remaining slices. Cover with baking (parchment) paper, place the colander over a deep bowl and weigh the covered eggplant down with a heavy object. Let it drain for at least 20 minutes, then sparingly pat down each slice with a paper towel and discard the water.

2 To fry the eggplant, coat the slices in flour on both sides (the moisture will help it stick) and place on a tray. Heat a generous amount of oil in a frying pan until it reaches 180°C (360°F) or small bubbles appear around the handle of a wooden spoon.

3 Fry the eggplant in batches, turning often, for a few minutes, or until golden brown. Transfer to a plate lined with paper towel, layering additional towels between slices to absorb excess oil.

4 Preheat the oven to 180°C (360°F).

5 To assemble the parmigiana, spread a thin layer of sugo in a baking dish, then arrange half the eggplant slices snugly side by side until the sugo is covered. Trim pieces if needed – it's a delicious jigsaw puzzle!

6 Add a third of the remaining sugo, then scatter a couple of torn basil leaves, Pecorino and half the mozzarella on top. Repeat layering with the remaining eggplant, sugo, basil and cheeses, pressing gently. For the final layer, use sugo only (no basil or cheese).

7 Cover with foil and bake for 30 minutes. Remove the foil and bake for another 10 minutes. Sprinkle Pecorino on top and return to the oven for 10 more minutes to melt. Leave it to set for 10–15 minutes before you slice into it, otherwise it'll be a soupy mess.

VINCENZO'S TIPS

- To prevent excess liquid, tear or dice the mozzarella, place it in a colander over a dish, cover the colander and refrigerate. Prepare this the night before cooking.
- Instead of frying the eggplant slices, you can bake them, which gives a firmer texture. Lightly brush with olive oil then bake on a lined baking tray at 220°C (430°C) for 30–35 minutes or until lightly golden and tender. Turn midway through.

BRACIOLE ALLA CALABRESE CALABRESE STUFFED MEAT ROLLS

Oh yes, Mamma Maria's Braciole alla Calabrese. Each one always perfectly rolled, with just the right amount of filling. Watching her make them is a treasured memory, a simple act that brings a great deal of happiness. *Braciole* are thin cuts of beef stuffed with cheese, eggplant, and salty prosciutto, then braised slowly in a rich tomato sugo. When you slice through one, you see every single layer. And when topped with a spoonful of sugo, it's a mouthful that feels like home. These are a favourite in southern Italy, especially in Calabria, where each family adds their own touch.

MAKES 4

2 medium eggplants (aubergines)
salt and pepper
4 veal fillets, thinly sliced
8 thin slices Italian prosciutto crudo
4 thin slices provolone cheese
150g (5.3 oz) baby spinach leaves
1/3 cup (80 ml/2.7 fl oz) extra virgin olive oil (EVOO)
1 garlic clove, crushed
1/4 brown or red onion, finely chopped
1 medium carrot, finely chopped
bunch of basil
400g (14.1 oz) store-bought passata or use homemade (see recipe, page 74)
grated Pecorino Romano, qb

SPECIAL EQUIPMENT
meat mallet
cooking string or twine (or use toothpicks)

METHOD

1 Trim the top and bottom of each eggplant, then slice lengthways into 1cm (1/2 inch) thick pieces. Lay on the chopping board, sprinkle with salt and let sit for 5 minutes.

2 Heat a grill or skillet over medium–high heat with a little EVOO, then pat dry the eggplant with paper towel to remove excess moisture. Grill in batches to avoid overcrowding, until lightly golden and slightly charred on one side, then flip and cook the other side. Transfer to a plate to rest.

3 Place the veal slices between sheets of baking (parchment) paper on a chopping board and flatten them gently with the flat side of a meat mallet, then season with salt and pepper. Repeat with remaining slices.

4 Layer 1 veal slice with 1 slice of each eggplant, prosciutto and provolone and some baby spinach. Don't overfill, to ensure they close properly. Gently fold the veal over the filling, tucking in the ends and pressing any spilling ingredients back in. Then roll up tightly and tie one end with cooking string, knotting to hold it in place. Wrap the string around the veal every 3cm (1.2 inches), looping and knotting tightly at the end. If you don't have string, toothpicks work too. Repeat until all the ingredients are used.

5 Heat the EVOO in a large frying pan and shallow-fry the rolls, turning with tongs until browned on all sides. Remove the rolls from the pan and rest for a few minutes to allow the juices to redistribute.

6 Add the garlic to the pan and, once golden, add the onion, carrot and a few basil leaves, letting it simmer for 5–7 minutes, or until the carrot starts to soften. Add the passata, more basil (reserving some for the garnish), then season. Mix and simmer, stirring occasionally, for 7 minutes or until the sauce thickens slightly.

7 Add the rolls to the sauce, coating them well with a spoon. Simmer, turning every few minutes, for 20 minutes, or until cooked through. Remove each roll with tongs and remove the string/toothpicks. Slice the rolls into bite-sized pieces and rest for 2–3 minutes to keep them juicy. Sprinkle with Pecorino, and serve.

MAMMA MARIA'S TIPS
- The veal needs to be thin but not so thin that it tears during rolling.
- Experiment with different fillings. Try pine nuts or a hint of lemon zest for a twist on the traditional recipe.

MINESTRONE HEARTY ITALIAN SOUP

Minestrone is our family's secret weapon – a dish always waiting in the freezer for those days when the clock is against us or the pantry looks bare. We make a big batch, ready for a quick and comforting meal that even our eldest son will devour, vegetables and all. Then there's the age-old debate of whether to add pasta or not. Vincenzo insists on it, but I find the thick, brothy texture perfect on its own. And that's the beauty of Minestrone: you can truly make it yours. Feel free to use whatever vegetables you have on hand, turning a few simple ingredients into a deeply satisfying bowl of goodness.

SERVES 6, WITH LEFTOVERS

extra virgin olive oil (EVOO), qb
1 celery stalk, finely chopped
1 red onion, finely chopped
2 carrots, finely chopped
4 rosemary sprigs
300g (10.6 oz) pumpkin, chopped into 2cm (½ inch) pieces
2 white potatoes, chopped into small pieces
800g (14.1 oz) canned diced Italian tomatoes
Parmigiano Reggiano rind, cut into cubes (optional)
1 broccoli head, chopped into small florets
salt and pepper
400g (14.1 oz) can mixed beans
400g (14.1 oz) can lentils
small bunch of flat-leaf (Italian) parsley, leaves finely chopped
300g (10.6 oz) ditalini or tubetti pasta (optional)
finely grated Pecorino Romano, to serve

METHOD

1 Heat an extra-large saucepan or stockpot over medium heat. Pour in a generous amount of EVOO. Add celery, onion and carrot. Strip leaves from 2–3 rosemary sprigs and toss them in. Add ⅓ cup water and stir with a wooden spoon. Cover and simmer, stirring occasionally, for 10 minutes, or until the soffritto has softened.

2 Add the pumpkin and potato, mix well, then drizzle in 80–100ml (2.7–3.4 fl oz) EVOO. Cook for 2 minutes, then pour in enough water to cover the ingredients (about 4 cups). Cover and cook over medium heat for 10–15 minutes.

3 Uncover, stir gently, then add the tomato and mix. Pour in another 3 cups water (or enough to cover all the ingredients). Add Parmigiano rind, a rosemary sprig, broccoli and a generous sprinkle of salt and pepper. If the broccoli isn't fully covered, add more water. Stir, cover and cook, stirring occasionally, for another 10 minutes.

4 Add the beans and lentils, mix through and sprinkle with ½ cup parsley. Pour in ½ cup water (or enough to cover all ingredients), stir and cook over medium–high heat for 20 minutes, stirring every so often. After 15 minutes, remove lid and use a wooden spoon to mix, scraping the bottom to ensure nothing sticks. Do this a few times so the ingredients really move around. Add another 2 cups water to ensure everything is submerged and stir a few more times for 5 minutes.

5 If skipping pasta, reduce heat to medium–low and cook for another 30 minutes, or until the liquid reduces slightly. If adding pasta, taste the veggies for tenderness, adjust salt if needed, then drizzle generously with EVOO and add pasta. Cook for 2–3 minutes less than the packet instructions, stirring often (lid off) and scraping the bottom to prevent sticking. The soup should bubble and boil as it cooks. Remove from heat.

6 Serve garnished with Pecorino, pepper and the remaining parsley.

VINCENZO'S TIPS
- Try to cut all the vegetables roughly the same size so they all cook evenly.
- Don't be shy with the water. Add more if needed – extra is better than not enough. While you can use vegetable stock, slow-cooking the veggies in water creates its own delicious stock, so there's really no need!
- This is a large batch. If you are preparing to have leftovers, cook the pasta separately, then add it in, or else it will overcook and break up when you reheat it, and reduce the liquid considerably.
- Store leftovers in airtight containers for the next day or freeze for up to 8 months. When reheating, do so in a saucepan and add a touch of water.

STINCO DI AGNELLO SLOW-COOKED LAMB SHANKS

This dish is pure, fall-off-the-bone, uncomplicated wonderfulness. It is so finger-licking good, our eldest son ate an entire lamb shank entirely by himself for his first birthday lunch (it was also during a Covid lockdown and undeniably the highlight of his year). Do not go past this one. It's fuss free and, after a quick sear, you can simply leave it to slow-cook. The hardest part about it is having patience! Once the aroma fills your kitchen, it'll be a true test of willpower to see how long you can hold off before dipping a crusty piece of bread into that irresistible sauce for a taste test!

SERVES 3
- 100ml (3.4 fl oz) extra virgin olive oil (EVOO)
- ½ brown onion, finely chopped
- 1 celery stalk, finely chopped
- 1 large carrot, finely chopped
- 3 top-quality lamb shanks
- 250ml (8.4 fl oz) vegetable stock
- 2 × 700g (47.3 fl oz) bottles tomato passata or use homemade (see recipe, page 74)
- salt and pepper
- bunch of flat-leaf (Italian) parsley, leaves chopped

SPECIAL EQUIPMENT
large cast-iron Dutch oven (or use a large saucepan with a lid)

METHOD

1 Heat the EVOO in a large cast-iron Dutch oven (or large saucepan with a lid) over medium–high heat, ensuring the bottom of the pot is evenly coated. Add the onion, celery and carrot, stirring with a wooden spoon to coat them well. Cover with the lid and let cook for 5 minutes, or until softened.

2 Remove the lid, stir the soffritto and add the lamb shanks, one at a time. Sear the sides of each one for 3–4 minutes, using tongs to turn them until they're evenly browned. This step builds rich flavour – don't rush it! If they're browning too quickly, lower the heat, aiming for golden, not burnt.

3 Pour in the stock, cover with the lid and cook, stirring occasionally, over medium–low heat for 10 minutes. Add the passata, then rinse the bottle with a little water to get every last drop, and pour it in. Season generously with salt and pepper, then stir to combine. Make sure the sauce completely coats the lamb shanks.

4 Cover the pan and cook over low heat for 3–4 hours, letting the shanks braise until they're irresistibly tender and falling off the bone. Every 30 minutes, stir and turn the shanks, ensuring they soak up all the rich, tomato goodness.

5 When serving, spread a generous scoop of the luscious sugo on the bottom of each serving plate, place a shank on top and smother it with more sauce. Garnish with parsley, and don't be shy about digging in – this is a dish meant for licking fingers and wiping plates clean!

VINCENZO'S TIPS
- A cast-iron pot really is the secret for a perfect golden sear and steady simmer. If you don't have one, use the large saucepan you usually choose for slow-cooking a sauce.
- Have leftover sauce? Toss it with pasta the next day or freeze it for up to 6 months for a quick meal when you are craving a bold, hearty sugo. You can thank me later!

POLLO ALLA CACCIATORA CHICKEN CACCIATORE

This is such a typical way for an Italian dish to carry its history in its name, telling a story before you've even taken a bite. The word *cacciatore* means 'hunter' in Italian, and this dish's origins are as flavourful as its ingredients. Traditionally, hunters would prepare this meal with wildfowl they'd caught themselves, picking up tomatoes and herbs they found along the way and adding a splash of wine from their supplies. After years of sharing this recipe online, we've seen it become a favourite for so many families, and it is scrumptious enough for even our youngest eaters to enjoy.

SERVES 6–8

- 1/3 cup (80ml/2.7 fl oz) extra virgin olive oil (EVOO)
- 4 chicken drumsticks
- 5 chicken wings
- 5 chicken thighs
- 2 garlic cloves
- 2 carrots, finely chopped
- 1/2 brown onion, finely chopped
- 1 celery stalk, finely chopped
- 1 rosemary sprig
- 150ml (5 oz) red wine
- 700g (24.7 oz) bottle tomato passata or use homemade (see recipe, page 74)
- salt and pepper
- bunch of flat-leaf (Italian) parsley, leaves finely chopped
- fresh thyme sprigs, to garnish (optional)

METHOD

1 Heat the EVOO in a large flameproof casserole dish or deep sauté pan over medium–low heat. Add the chicken and braise for 5 minutes on each side or until golden brown, working in batches if necessary.

2 Return all the chicken to the dish. Throw in the garlic cloves whole, then cover and cook for a few minutes. Flip each piece of chicken, cover and cook for another 10 minutes.

3 Add the carrot, onion and celery, ensuring everything is evenly distributed. Cover and cook for 10 minutes or until the vegetables become tender.

4 Mix in the rosemary and wine and cover. Cook for 10 minutes, then remove the lid, flip the chicken and cook for a few more minutes or until the wine evaporates. Stir through the passata, season with salt and pepper, then stir in a handful of parsley. Cover and cook for 10 minutes to develop the flavour, then remove the rosemary sprigs and garlic cloves.

5 Finish by cooking, uncovered, for another 10 minutes, then sprinkle with the remaining parsley and thyme (if using) before serving.

VINCENZO'S TIPS
- You can use any part of the chicken for this recipe, including breasts, wings or thighs (bones in or removed). It is most commonly served with drumsticks.
- The alcohol cooks off, leaving just the rich flavour. If wine isn't your thing, chicken stock or water make great substitutes.
- Pollo alla cacciatora is all about improvising with what you've got. Toss in olives, mushrooms or other vegetables you love.
- Cooking this dish low and slow is crucial to keeping the chicken moist. Patience is key – good things take time to develop their best flavours.

LE POLPETTE ITALIAN MEATBALLS

For Vincenzo, meatballs – *polpette* – are so much more than a dish. Vincenzo grew up with different versions and was determined to create his own family recipe of tender, juicy, flavoursome morsels. Over the years, he's made a few tweaks to elevate the flavour even more, creating a dish so good that no one can resist it. We once sold thousands at an Italian festival, topped with creamy burrata. Don't settle for a small portion – these are meant to be eaten as a main meal (and definitely not with pasta!).

MAKES 24–30
1/4 brown onion, halved
1/2 carrot, halved crossways
1/2 celery stalk, halved in the middle, leaves discarded
extra virgin olive oil (EVOO), qb
4 slices Italian, artisan or sourdough bread, crusts left on
500g (17.6 oz) minced (ground) pork
500g (17.6 oz) minced (ground) beef or veal
5 tbsp finely grated Pecorino Romano or Parmigiano Reggiano, plus extra to serve
3 tbsp fresh or dried breadcrumbs
1 tbsp salt
pepper
1 egg
2 garlic cloves, crushed
bunch of flat-leaf (Italian) parsley, leaves finely chopped
Tomato and basil sugo (see recipe, page 60)
burrata, to serve (optional)

SPECIAL EQUIPMENT
immersion blender

METHOD

1 Blend the onion, carrot and celery with 2–3 tablespoons of EVOO and a splash of water at medium–high speed for 1 minute, or until thick and creamy. Soak the bread in a bowl of warm water and set aside.

2 In a large bowl, combine the minces, breaking them down using your hands. Add the blended soffritto, cheese, breadcrumbs, salt, pepper, egg, garlic and parsley. Squeeze excess water from the bread, then break it into small pieces and add to the mixture. Mix thoroughly until combined, then wash your hands.

3 Moisten your hands with water (keep a bowl nearby to use as needed). Scoop a tablespoon of the mixture, press it between your hands and roll it into a meatball of your preferred size. Place it on a tray lined with baking (parchment) paper and repeat with the remaining mixture. If you are freezing them, place uncooked in the freezer in an airtight container and use within 3 months.

4 There are three ways to cook these meatballs – choose which suits your tastebuds!

To bake: Preheat the oven to 180°C (360°F). Bake for 15 minutes, or until lightly golden. Warm the sauce in a saucepan, then transfer the meatballs to the pan. Cover and simmer over low heat for 30 minutes, stirring gently every 5–10 minutes.

To shallow-fry: Heat a generous amount of EVOO in a large frying pan over medium heat. Add the meatballs in batches, ensuring you don't overcrowd the pan, and fry for about 5 minutes, turning each one to brown all over. Warm the sauce in a saucepan, then transfer the meatballs to the pan. Cover and simmer over low heat for 30 minutes, or until moist and cooked through.

To cook from frozen (Vincenzo's favoured method): Heat the sauce in a saucepan over medium–low heat until piping hot, then add the frozen meatballs directly to the pan, ensuring they are fully submerged. Cover and simmer for 40 minutes in total. For the first 10 minutes move the pan around in a circular motion gently, rather than using a utensil to stir them. You can then use a spoon to move them around for the remaining time while the meatballs soften and cook through.

5 To serve, spoon some sugo onto a serving plate, then top with meatballs and more sauce. For something different, top with a burrata, then slice through it once served so it slides down and smothers the meatballs.

VINCENZO'S TIP
- When mixing the meatballs in the sugo, swirl the pan to coat them in the sauce rather than using a utensil to combine, as they can easily break. Check the meatballs are cooked by slicing one in half.

COTOLETTA DELLA NONNA IGEA NONNA'S SCHNITZEL

With hardly any ingredients and just a few steps, you'll have dinner made and your freezer stocked (just increase the quantity). These crispy cutlets are an example of what is whipped up in an Italian household when hunger strikes and there is little time to spare. Literally no household can be without these in their freezer. They are often prepared to enjoy alongside a salad as a light meal, after a hearty primo, or for the *nipoti* (grandchildren) when they arrive at Nonna's unexpectedly and she hasn't prepared! Pair with comforting sides like crispy roasted potatoes and a fennel and lettuce salad.

SERVES 4

3 eggs
salt
juice of ½ lemon
fresh breadcrumbs, for coating (see tips, page 146)
4 unbreaded chicken breast or veal schnitzel fillets (chicken is Nonna's preference)
sunflower or olive oil, for shallow-frying

METHOD

1 Crack the eggs into a bowl and whisk well with a pinch of salt and the juice of half a lemon. Nonna swears by this clever trick – just a squeeze of lemon keeps the meat from having an eggy smell. Mix thoroughly to combine. Fill a separate bowl with breadcrumbs.

2 Sprinkle a small amount of salt on both sides of each fillet. Dip the meat into the egg mixture, ensuring the fillets are fully coated. Use a fork to turn them over and coat evenly.

3 Place each fillet on the breadcrumbs, pressing down firmly so the breadcrumbs stick. Flip and repeat to ensure both sides are covered beautifully. Transfer them to a flat plate, cover and place in the fridge to rest while you heat the oil (see Nonna Igea's tip below).

4 Pour enough oil into a frying pan so that the oil is about 3cm (1.2 inch) deep and heat over medium heat. Test to see if the oil is hot enough by dropping a few breadcrumbs in. Once they start to sizzle, the oil is ready. Gently place the schnitzels into the pan. Fry them for 3–4 minutes per side, or until crispy and golden.

5 To keep these schnitzels perfectly crispy, drain any excess oil once cooked, then serve them right away.

NONNA IGEA'S TIPS
- After you coat the meat, let it rest for a few minutes – don't rush! This way, the crumbs stick nicely and nothing falls apart when you fry it. If you're planning ahead, you can even pop the fillets in the fridge overnight, covered, and they will be perfect when you're ready.
- *Cotolette* freeze really well, so freeze them in a single layer after coating them with breadcrumbs but before frying. Once frozen, transfer them to an airtight container for up to 6 months. Thaw in the fridge overnight before cooking.

SCRIPPELLE 'MBUSSE DELLA NONNA IGEA
CREPES IN BROTH FROM TERAMO

It might sound like an unlikely combination, but Nonna's crepes and *brodo* come together to create this surprising-yet-ideal match. The first time I tasted this, I closed my eyes after that first bite. I couldn't help it. It was as if I'd been transported to a place of pure bliss, with my every worry melting away. At that moment, I was reminded of the true power of cooking and sharing recipes. I'd initially doubted I would like this dish, but after my first bowl I couldn't help but think how fortunate we were to nourish our bodies with simple, nutrient-dense recipes from generations past – a time when life was simpler and the most important part of the day was gathering around the table with loved ones. Even our photographer, who like me initially questioned the dish, has been raving about its flavours ever since she took her first bite.

SERVES 6
24 freshly made crepes, cooled (see recipe, page 114)
grated Parmigiano Reggiano

BRODO DELLA NONNA IGEA (NONNA'S BROTH)
½ chicken, cut into pieces
5 small veal cutlets or chops, bones in
1 whole brown onion, peeled
1 carrot, peeled, halved crossways
3 celery stalks, halved crossways, with leaves intact
4 cherry tomatoes
1 cinnamon stick (not ground!)
rock salt

METHOD

1 To make the broth, place the chicken and veal in a large saucepan or stockpot and fill it almost to the top with water. Cover with a lid and bring it to the boil over medium heat.

2 Once it boils, remove the lid and, when it creates a thick foam on top, skim it off using a slotted spoon and discard. Continue to boil for another 10 minutes, before removing the foam once again.

3 Add the onion, carrot, celery, tomatoes, cinnamon stick and a generous pinch of rock salt. Cover and cook over medium–low heat for up to 2 hours, or until the meat is tender. Once it is ready you will notice the water level has dropped.

4 Lay a crepe on your work surface and sprinkle with Parmigiano. Roll it up gently and tightly, then turn it so that the edge is at the bottom, and place in a serving bowl. Repeat with the remaining crepes, placing 4 crepes in each serving bowl, arranged tightly next to one another in one direction.

5 Using a ladle, scoop out the broth and pour it through a sieve into a clean bowl to remove the solids. Then ladle some of the clear broth into each bowl of crepes.

6 Add another sprinkle of Parmigiano to each bowl and enjoy hot, breaking into the crepes with a spoon and scooping them up with some broth so every mouthful is filled with both.

NONNA IGEA'S TIPS
- If you soak the meat and any bones in water overnight before making soup, you'll find there's less foam to skim off the top during cooking.
- You can use beef instead of veal; just remember to adjust the cooking time as needed. Beef requires more time to become tender.
- Taste the broth every now and then during cooking and adjust the seasoning as necessary.

COZZE E VONGOLE MUSSELS AND CLAMS

This dish had to be in the book – it's a classic, so beloved that it even has its own song in Abruzzo. Every time our eldest son, Sebastian, hears it, his face lights up and he shares a laugh with Nonno Paolo, who would happily make this dish for him every day if he could. The beauty of Cozze e vongole lies in its simplicity – just mussels and clams, combined with cherry tomatoes, onion and white wine. The flavours transport you straight to the Adriatic. It's quick to make, and there's something wonderfully satisfying about slurping up mussels and clams in company!

SERVES 6
1kg (35.3 oz) vongole (clams)
sea salt
1.5kg (52.9 oz) mussels
250g (8.8 oz) cherry tomatoes, halved
½ brown onion, diced
100ml (3.4 fl oz) extra virgin olive oil (EVOO)
½ glass dry white wine
chopped flat-leaf (Italian) parsley leaves and fresh sourdough bread, to serve

METHOD

1 Fill a large clean bowl with cold water and add the vongole and 3 heaped tbsp sea salt. You want enough water to cover the vongole. Leave to soak for 4 hours, changing the water after 2 hours, to remove the most amount of grit and impurities. Strain any sand or grit using a colander and leave to the side.

2 Clean the mussels, following Nonno Paolo's tips below.

3 Sauté the tomato and onion with the EVOO in an extra-large saucepan or stockpot over medium–low heat for 10 minutes. Add the wine, mussels, vongole and a pinch of salt, then mix using a wooden spoon.

4 Cover with a lid and leave to steam and cook for 10 minutes, or until almost all the shells have opened.

5 Serve hot in a bowl garnished with a generous amount of parsley and a side of sourdough bread.

NONNO PAOLO'S TIPS
- It is essential to clean the mussels to ensure they are both safe and pleasant to eat. First discard any with broken shells or that stay open after a gentle tap. Only the freshest should make it to the pot. Then rinse the mussels under cold running water, rubbing off any dirt or sand. Firmly pull out the fibrous beard threads towards the hinge with a quick tug downwards and out. Then use a stiff brush or the back of a knife to scrub the shells and remove any barnacles, rough patches or debris. Finally, soak them in cold, salted water for 20 minutes to expel any grit, and rinse them one last time under cold water. Cook them the same day you clean them.
- If you don't have an extra-large saucepan or stockpot, you can cook this in batches or reduce the quantity.
- When this dish is ready it creates a beautiful broth-like liquid. If there is any left after you have mopped up with the bread, you can use it the next day to make pasta or a brothy soup with short pasta like ditalini.

DOLCI

DOLCI

A truly great Italian meal is incomplete without the grand finale: dessert. Or as Italians say, dolci. We are always drawn in by the irresistible pull of a pasticceria – those beautiful pastry shops brimming with sugary works of art.

From the mountainous north to the sun-drenched south, each Italian region boasts its own sweet specialties, many of which have been regarded as secrets by the older generations. In small towns and villages, the keepers of these recipes – often beloved nonnas – have carefully guarded these recipes, sharing them only with close family members. As a result, with time, many treasured sweet recipes have faded into memory. I've heard so many stories of cherished family recipes that were never written down, leaving families yearning for the flavours of their childhoods. This chapter (and pretty much our entire sense of being) is our homage to preserving a selection of those tastes.

The recipes we have chosen are a combination of family treasures and Italian classics. There's Nonna Igea's delicate Caggiunitt Abruzzesi – jam-stuffed fried ravioli that are a staple for festive occasions. And Bisnonno Tobia's Zabaglione, a silky, egg-rich dessert made with freshly gathered ingredients that Vincenzo remembers savouring during summers in Abruzzo. Then, of course, there's Vincenzo's Tiramisù – the version that converted even the sceptics (including me!) with its perfect balance of coffee, luscious mascarpone and cocoa. And no dessert chapter would be complete without Mamma Maria's Amaretti biscotti, a recipe so beloved it became the star of a market stand we hosted for several years and on our social media.

For Vincenzo, there's no better way to start the day than with something sweet – in his opinion, life's better that way. And when someone exclaims, 'Ohhh, it's too rich,' he always laughs and replies, 'Isn't that exactly what a dessert should be?'

CAGGIUNITT ABRUZZESI FRIED SWEET RAVIOLI

Caggiunitt Abruzzesi are Nonna Igea's delicate, crispy sweet ravioli filled with grape jam, toasted almonds and grated chocolate. Though they are typically made at Christmas, Nonna knows how quickly they disappear, so she makes them year-round for the family. Each bite offers a perfect contrast: thin, crispy pastry on the outside and a rich, sweet filling inside. Dusted with icing sugar, they're utterly irresistible. Passed down through generations, these sweet treats are a beloved family staple, and obviously we claim Nonna's version to be the best, so we're very happy to pass it on.

MAKES ABOUT 50

- 500g (17.6 oz) plain (all-purpose) flour, plus extra for dusting
- 1 egg yolk
- 100ml (3.4 fl oz) sunflower oil, plus extra, for deep-frying
- 1 tsp sugar
- pinch of salt
- 200–250ml (6.7–8.4 fl oz) white wine, plus extra if needed
- ½ glass Marsala or mosto cotto, or fresh espresso coffee, slightly cooled
- icing sugar, for dusting

CHOCOLATE GRAPE FILLING

- 250g (9 oz) grape jam (or your preferred flavour)
- 300g (10.6 oz) crushed toasted almonds, peeled
- ½ tsp sugar
- 15–30ml (0.5–1 fl oz) fresh espresso coffee, chilled
- 200g (7 oz) dark chocolate, grated

SPECIAL EQUIPMENT

- pasta machine
- ravioli cutter

METHOD

1 To make the chocolate grape filling, combine all filling ingredients in a bowl. Mix well and set aside.

2 On a clean surface, mound the plain flour and create a well in the centre, then add the egg yolk, and beat gently before pouring in the sunflower oil, and adding the sugar and salt. Mix well using your hands. Gradually add the wine, mixing until the dough begins to soften and come together. If it is soft enough, you do not need to use it all up. Knead for 6-8 minutes until smooth and soft. Gradually add the marsala (or mosto cotto or coffee) until the dough no longer feels dry.

3 Cover with a large bowl, ensuring no air gets inside. Dust your work surface with extra flour, then remove the bowl from the dough and cut a small portion to begin shaping. Cover the remaining dough again so it doesn't dry out.

4 Set your pasta machine to the thickest setting. Flatten the dough slightly with your hands, then run it through the machine two to three times. Gradually thin the dough by moving down the dial and running it through each setting until you have a long, smooth strip.

5 Place small spoonfuls of the filling along the bottom half of the dough, spacing about 2 finger-widths apart. Carefully fold the dough over the filling. Press to seal and remove any air pockets. Use a ravioli cutter to trim and separate each piece, placing them on a flour-dusted tray. Repeat until you have used all your dough.

6 Heat a generous amount of oil in a frying pan until it reaches 180°C (360°F) or small bubbles appear around the handle of a wooden spoon. Once hot, fry 5–7 ravioli at a time, turning gently for even cooking. When golden and crispy, use a slotted spatula to transfer the ravioli to a paper-towel-lined tray to drain excess oil and cool slightly. Transfer to a plate and dust with icing sugar.

NONNA IGEA'S TIPS

- Keep the sweet ravioli mostly uniform in size to ensure each one is cooked evenly, golden and crisp.
- Test the oil temperature with a small piece of dough, by dropping it in once you think it is hot enough. It should sizzle without burning.
- Don't overcrowd the pan. Fry in batches instead to maintain the oil temperature for crisp results.
- Above all, share with loved ones. Even if the ravioli don't turn out perfect, it doesn't matter; enjoying them together is the best part.

TIRAMISÙ

I thought I'd tasted a pretty decent tiramisù and still, never really loved it – until Vincenzo made me his. The moment I took my first bite, I knew I'd been wrong all along. This isn't just a dessert, it's a decadent experience. Each layer is meticulously crafted with love and care, blending creamy mascarpone, espresso-soaked savoiardi, and a dusting of cocoa that's like sprinkles of pure magic. It's rich, but not too heavy. Bold, but balanced. A little indulgent, yet completely irresistible. Trust me – once you try Vincenzo's tiramisù, you'll realise it's the standard by which all others should be judged. No more settling for lacklustre versions.

SERVES 8–10
5 eggs
5 tbsp white (granulated) sugar
500g (17.6 oz) mascarpone
400g (14.1 oz) savoiardi (ladyfinger) biscuits
700ml (23.7 fl oz) fresh Italian coffee/espresso, cooled to room temperature
cocoa powder, for dusting
a few squares of dark or white chocolate, grated, plus extra, to serve (optional)

SPECIAL EQUIPMENT
electric hand mixer
22 × 33cm (9 × 13 inch) deep glass baking dish

METHOD

1 Separate the egg yolks and egg whites into two mixing bowls. Using an electric hand mixer or stand mixer, beat the yolks on medium speed, then increase to high speed for about 20 seconds.

2 Add 1 tbsp of sugar to the yolk bowl and mix again until most of the bubbles disappear. Keep mixing until the yolks are thick, scraping the bottom of the bowl as you go. Add the mascarpone and mix gently on medium speed, gradually increasing the speed and scraping the bottom until smooth. Set aside.

3 Next, beat the egg whites, starting on medium speed until they begin to foam. Add the remaining sugar one tablespoon at a time (gradually), mixing well after each addition. Once all the sugar is added, increase to high speed and keep mixing for about 2 minutes, until the mixture is creamy and foamy, but not overly bubbly. Fold the egg whites into the yolk mixture using a spatula. Do this gently so the mixture stays fluffy.

4 Dip each biscuit in the coffee for 2–3 seconds, keeping them flat and letting the excess drip off. Arrange them sugar-side down in a single layer in the base of the baking dish, filling any gaps with smaller pieces.

5 Spread a layer of mascarpone cream evenly over the biscuits, covering all edges and corners. Then sift cocoa powder generously over the cream until it is completely covered and sprinkle the grated chocolate sparingly on top. Add another coffee-dipped biscuit layer, aligned with the first, and spread the mascarpone mixture evenly on top.

6 Sift cocoa powder over the top again, along with grated chocolate (if using) and repeat one more layer if it fits into your tray. For the final layer, spread the remaining cream evenly on top of the biscuits then gently shake the tray slightly to help it settle, sifting more cocoa powder over the top until no white is showing. Cover and refrigerate for at least 4 hours, or 24 hours for best results.

7 Dust servings with extra cocoa and garnish with a piece of chocolate when serving.

VINCENZO'S TIPS
- For liqueur lovers, splash some amaretto or sambuca into your coffee before dipping the biscuits.
- Have leftover mascarpone mixture? Stir in fruit, like blackberries, and freeze for a quick homemade ice cream. If you're keeping it fresh, use it within 24 hours.
- You may have fewer portions if you're serving proper Italian portions. In that case, make a second tiramisù.
- Children, the elderly and people who are pregnant or have a compromised immune system should avoid eating this dish as it contains raw egg. To reduce any risks or if you are concerned, use an egg separator rather than egg halves to separate the yolks and whites, and eat this dish within one day of making it.

ZABAGLIONE ITALIAN-STYLE CUSTARD

For Vincenzo, zabaglione is a spoonful of childhood wrapped in love and tradition. He fondly remembers long summer days in Villa Petto, the small village in Teramo, Abruzzo, where his *bisnonni* (great grandparents) were from. When Vincenzo spent time there, Bisnonno Tobia would rise early to gather fresh eggs from the chickens and milk from the neighbouring farms. With simple, humble ingredients, he would transform the kitchen into a place of magic, whisking up this silky, cloud-like custard. It was more than just a treat – it was a quiet moment between them, a sweet pause in the day filled with laughter. While tradition calls for a splash of Marsala in zabaglione, when Vincenzo was little, Bisnonno would swap it out for milk ... or at least that's what he said. Maybe a drop or two still found its way in – after all, Vincenzo was always full of energy, and still is!

Whether you enjoy it for breakfast or as a dessert, this luscious blend of egg yolks, sugar and Marsala is comfort in its purest form – a taste of family, tradition and irreplaceable moments we long to pass on.

SERVES 3–6

5 egg yolks
1/3 cup (75g/2.6 oz) white (granulated) sugar
50ml (1.7 fl oz) Marsala, Frangelico or amaretto
berries, grated chocolate or finely grated citrus zest, for garnishing (optional)
savoiardi (ladyfinger) biscuits, to serve (optional)

SPECIAL EQUIPMENT
sugar thermometer

METHOD

1 Fill a medium saucepan three-quarters full with water and leave it to warm up, but not boil.

2 While the water heats up, vigorously whisk the egg yolks in a heatproof bowl using either a whisk or an electric hand mixer. Gradually add the sugar, one third at a time, whisking until the mixture becomes creamy.

3 Once the water boils, reduce the heat to a simmer and place the bowl over the pan, allowing it to just touch the surface of the water, without it being submerged.

4 Whisk the egg mixture continuously, adding your choice of liqueur in two batches. Keep whisking until the mixture thickens to a cream-like consistency and fine lines form when you lift the whisk. Continue this process for 6-10 minutes, checking the water every so often to make sure it is not boiling aggressively under the bowl. A gentle bubble is fine. Use a sugar thermometer to check the temperature of the zabaglione mixture – it should reach 70°C (160°F).

5 Turn off the heat and pour the zabaglione equally between either 3 martini glasses or 6 shot glasses. It can be served warm while still runny or cold once the mixture thickens (which many prefer). Garnish with berries, grated chocolate or citrus zest. Add a biscuit, crumbled into pieces, for crunch. Remember, this dessert is rich, so small portions are ideal!

VINCENZO'S TIPS

- Use the leftover egg whites for Mamma Maria's Amaretti (see recipe, page 227).
- The *bagnomaria* (bain-marie/double-boiler) method gently cooks the egg yolks, preventing them from scrambling.
- If you want to avoid alcohol, boil the liqueur separately before adding – it retains the flavour while evaporating the alcohol. You could also substitute the alcohol for a splash of vanilla bean extract, or for an Italian-style breakfast treat, replace the alcohol with milk and honey.

BISCOTTI DI MANDORLA ALMOND BISCUITS

This recipe is my mamma Maria's version of the beloved Italian cantucci. Whether these crunchy, nutty treats are dunked into coffee, served with tea or dipped into a glass of *vin santo* (a dessert wine from Tuscany that translates to 'holy wine'), it's hard not to devour several in one sitting. The biscotti are wonderfully fragrant, with a hint of zesty lemon. They're just as delightful to bake as they are to eat. Who says the Italians haven't thought of everything? I mean, dipping biscotti into wine? Yes please!

MAKES 40–50
200g (7 oz) caster (superfine) sugar
2 eggs
1 tsp vanilla extract
zest of 1 lemon
250g (8.8 oz) plain (all-purpose) flour, plus extra for dusting
½ tsp baking powder
150g (5.3 oz) whole almonds (roasted if preferred)

SPECIAL EQUIPMENT
hand mixer

METHOD

1 Preheat the oven to 180°C (360°F) and line a tray with baking (parchment) paper.

2 In a bowl, combine the sugar, eggs, vanilla and lemon zest. Beat with a hand mixer on medium speed for 4 minutes, or until light and fluffy.

3 Add the flour, baking powder and almonds. Mix with a spatula or your hands, adding a little extra flour if needed until the dough comes together.

4 Turn the dough onto a floured surface and knead gently. Once it has come together well, divide it into 2 portions and roll each into a log shape. Place the logs on the prepared tray, leaving space between them. Bake for 20–25 minutes, or until golden.

5 Remove from the oven and cool for 30 minutes. Lower the oven to 140°C (285°F).

6 Once cooled, use a serrated knife to slice the logs at an angle into biscotti shapes of your preferred size. Place back on the tray, cut side up, and bake for 10 minutes. Flip and bake for another 10 minutes, until golden and crisp. Cool completely on a wire rack.

MAMMA MARIA'S TIPS
- For added sweetness, add chocolate chips to the dough along with the almonds.
- You can substitute the lemon zest with orange zest, and almonds with pistachios or walnuts.
- If the dough is too soft to roll out, an extra dusting of flour will really help.
- These can be stored in an airtight container in the pantry for up to 2 weeks.

LIMONCELLO DELLA NONNA IGEA

For decades, Nonna Igea has been perfecting her limoncello, a liquid sunshine, loved and shared in homes around the world. From small bottles prepared for a special celebration to a chilled glass poured 'just because', her recipe has become a treasured ritual for countless people. And for good reason. This version hits the mark every single time. Made with three simple ingredients – the skin of the finest lemons, pure sugar, and alcohol – this limoncello is a game of patience. Nonna's process hinges on waiting for the flavours to fully infuse and transform into a vibrant, perfectly balanced liqueur with just the right amount of zest and strength. Try it, and bottle it with love, just like Nonna does; it makes all the difference. (Warning: once enjoyed, it can encourage laughter!)

MAKES 12 CUPS (3L/101.4 FL OZ)
9 organic lemons, washed thoroughly
4 cups (1L/33.8 fl oz) pure grain alcohol
700g (24.7 oz) white (granulated) sugar

SPECIAL EQUIPMENT
1 large jar with a lid
3 sterilised 1L bottles for your finished product
kitchen funnel

METHOD

1 Peel the lemons carefully using a peeler, making sure to remove just the skin, not the white pith, which can impart a bitter flavour.

2 Place the lemon skins in a large jar and add the alcohol. Press the skins down so they are completely submerged in the alcohol. Seal the jar tightly with a lid and let it infuse for 20 days in a cool, dark place, shaking the bottle every so often.

3 After 20 days, bring 6 cups water to the boil in a saucepan and add the sugar, mixing until it is completely dissolved. Remove from the heat and, once the mixture cools completely, strain the lemon-infused alcohol into the water using a colander or muslin (cheesecloth) to remove the lemon skins.

4 To extract any remaining flavour, pour a glass (no more than 250ml) of water into the jar the alcohol was in and shake it well, then strain this into the pan too. Mix well using a wooden spoon.

5 Pour the limoncello into sterilised bottles using a funnel and store one in the fridge and the rest in a cool, dry place. If using pure alcohol, it can also be stored in the freezer.

NONNA IGEA'S TIPS

- If you can't find pure grain alcohol, you can use 190-proof (95% ABV) Everclear, but it will result in a milder flavour. Avoid using vodka as it will not give you the right result. To enhance the lemon taste, you can infuse it longer, or adjust the sugar slightly – add more for a sweeter result, or decrease for a sourer flavour.
- To make a sweet, creamy version, called Crema di limoncello, follow the same process but reduce the infusing time to 15 days. Replace the water with 8 cups (2L/67.6 fl oz) full cream milk, boiling it for 20 minutes and skimming the first layer of foam as it forms. Once boiling, add 1kg (2 lb 3 oz) of white (granulated) sugar and stir until dissolved. After the mixture has completely cooled,, add ½ tsp vanilla powder or extract, then mix in the lemon-infused alcohol, passing it through a colander of muslin. This mixture can then be transferred into bottles using a funnel. It is best kept in the fridge for up to 6 months, or the freezer for up to 12 months.

PANNA COTTA

Vincenzo's version of panna cotta isn't just creamy, it's transformative. Each spoonful has a jiggly texture, subtle sweetness and delicate vanilla notes that all come together in perfect harmony. Over the years, even those who have been reluctant to try this wobbly delight have become panna cotta fans, and they always end up begging for the recipe. Once you try this classic, you'll see why it stands out. And the best part is you can personalise it every time, depending on your mood or the season – whether it's with fresh berries, a drizzle of chocolate or a swirl of tangy fruit coulis.

SERVES 4
9g gelatine leaves (about 5 small, platinum-strength leaves)
300ml (10.1 fl oz) full fat cream
90g (3.2 oz) white (granulated) sugar
1 tbsp vanilla extract or 1 vanilla pod, split, seeds scraped
blueberries and mint leaves, to garnish (optional)

STRAWBERRY COULIS
250g (8.8 oz) strawberries, washed, hulled and cut into quarters
50g (1.7 oz) white (granulated) sugar

SPECIAL EQUIPMENT
food processor or handheld blender
silicone moulds or ramekins (optional)

METHOD

1 Submerge the gelatine leaves in a bowl of room-temperature water for 5–7 minutes, letting them bloom (expand) and go wrinkly.

2 In a saucepan, gently warm up the cream over medium–low heat until small bubbles form around the edge, but don't let it boil. Mix in the sugar, stirring gently with a spatula, until dissolved. Add the vanilla and stir to combine. Once small bubbles form around the edge again, remove the pan from the heat. Remove the vanilla pod if using.

3 Squeeze any excess water from the softened gelatine using your hands and add the gelatine to the hot cream mixture, stirring continuously, until the gelatine fully dissolves and there are no lumps.

4 Pour the mixture into 4 silicone moulds or serving glasses. Cool completely before refrigerating for at least 4 hours to set, or overnight for best results.

5 For the strawberry coulis, combine the strawberry, sugar and 2 tbsp water in a small saucepan over medium heat. Simmer, stirring occasionally, for 5 minutes, or until the strawberry softens and the sugar dissolves. Remove from the heat and pour the mixture into a food processor. Pulse until smooth but still slightly thick. (Alternatively, use a handheld blender.) Transfer to a large glass or pitcher and refrigerate.

6 Check the panna cotta has set by gently tilting the glass or mould. Invert onto a plate if in moulds or ramekins. To serve, top with the strawberry coulis and garnish with blueberries and mint, if using.

VINCENZO'S TIPS

- If gelatine leaves are hard to source, substitute them with 2 tsp of gelatine powder. In this case, skip step 1 and in step 3 stir it into the hot cream mixture.
- To remove from the moulds or ramekins, run a thin butter knife around the inside edge to loosen. Prepare a tray with hot water and dip the mould or ramekin in for about 5 seconds to release the base. Place a plate on top, flip it over, and give a gentle tap so the dessert slides out.
- For an alternative topping, melt 200g dark chocolate with 1 cup (250ml/8.4 fl oz) cream in a small saucepan or double-boiler. Stir in 2 tbsp butter and a pinch of salt until smooth and glossy. But use any topping you like: fresh fruit, crushed biscuit and other fruit coulis are all delicious.

SBRICIOLATA ALLA RICOTTA E CIOCCOLATO
RICOTTA AND CHOCOLATE CRUMBLE

This isn't just any crumble; this is *sbriciolata*, the Italian twist on a classic dessert that somehow holds together, yet crumbles just the right way. Imagine this: a warm, golden crumble topping with its buttery crunch enveloping a smooth, rich ricotta and chocolate filling. Nearly two decades ago, when Vincenzo and I lived in Italy, Mamma Graziella's recipe was a favourite and our go-to dessert. We made it constantly, not just for family, but to share with friends too. In Italy, you always bring a treat when visiting someone – it's sacrilege to show up empty-handed!

SERVES 6–8
1 egg
100g (3.5 oz) white (granulated) sugar
zest of ½ lemon
2 cups (300g/10.6 oz) plain (all-purpose) flour
1 tsp bicarbonate (baking) soda
100g (3.5 oz) unsalted butter, softened but still with a slight firmness to it (otherwise the crumb won't form)
icing (confectioner's) sugar, for dusting

RICOTTA AND CHOCOLATE FILLING
500g (17.6 oz) ricotta
150g (5.3 oz) white (granulated) sugar
generous sprinkle of ground cinnamon, qb
finely grated zest of ½ lemon
100g (3.5 oz) dark chocolate, roughly chopped

SPECIAL EQUIPMENT
24cm (9.5 inch) round cake tin

METHOD

1 For the ricotta and chocolate filling, mix the ricotta and white sugar using a hand mixer or fork, depending on your desired texture. A mixer helps the sugar dissolve better. Stir in the cinnamon and lemon zest, then fold in the chocolate with a spoon. Set aside in the fridge.

2 In a bowl, beat the egg using a fork until well combined, then add the white sugar and mix until creamy. Stir in the lemon zest. Gradually add the flour and bicarb, mixing gently to combine.

3 Chop the butter into small pieces and add to the bowl. Using your hands, squeeze and press the mixture to incorporate the butter into the dry ingredients. Work it through until it forms uneven clumps, with some larger pieces, resembling crumble. Avoid overworking into tiny crumbs, as this will alter the texture.

4 Preheat the oven to 170°C (340°F). Prepare a round cake tin by lining the base and side with baking (parchment) paper or by greasing with butter and dusting with plain flour.

5 Sprinkle half the crumble mixture into the prepared tin to create an even base, covering it well and using any finer pieces of crumble to fill any gaps. Build the edge slightly higher to create a border.

6 Spread the ricotta filling over the base, keeping the surface smooth and away from the edge, to create a border all the way around, almost like the crust of a pizza. Cover with the remaining crumble mixture, ensuring the filling is completely hidden.

7 Bake for 30–40 minutes, turning the tin halfway for even cooking. Remove once the top is golden. Let it cool for 10 minutes before removing from the tin. Transfer to a wire rack to further cool and set before dusting with icing sugar and cutting into slices.

MAMMA GRAZIELLA'S TIPS
- When making the crumble, move the mixture around every now and then, almost scooping the bottom around to the top, so the fine crumble isn't all left at the bottom.
- Even though it will be hard, resist cutting the finished crumble while it's still hot – it'll crumble everywhere! Let it set and cool for perfect slices.
- Get creative with fillings: either jam or hazelnut spread will work well in place of the chocolate filling.

AMARETTI — AMARETTI BISCUITS

My mamma, Maria, has a signature treat and it's her amaretti. While many variations exist, even Vincenzo is pretty certain none come close to hers. These little bites of Italy have become synonymous with a visit to her home. They pair wonderfully with a rich espresso or a calming tea. Each bite is a satisfying contrast of crunchy edges and a soft, melt-in-your-mouth centre – exactly the way amaretti should be. What makes them truly special, though, is the care she pours into every batch. How she manages to make each one look exactly the same, I'll never know!

MAKES 20

5 egg whites, at room temperature
50ml (1.7fl oz) almond essence or extract
500g (17.6 oz) almond meal
300g (10.6 oz) caster (superfine) sugar
small bowl of icing (confectioner's) sugar, plus extra for dusting
glacé cherries (optional)

METHOD

1 Whisk the egg whites in a bowl until frothy. Add the almond essence and whisk well to combine.

2 In a separate bowl, mix the almond meal and caster sugar until the sugar seems to disappear.

3 Pour the egg white mixture over the dry ingredients and mix using a spoon. Once it starts binding, use your hands to mix until thoroughly combined. Don't try to form a ball – just gently compact the mixture in the bowl. Let it rest for up to 1 hour before rolling out the biscuits.

4 Preheat the oven to 180°C (360°F) and line a large baking tray with baking (parchment) paper.

5 Scoop a heaped teaspoon of the mixture and roll into a ball in your palms. Roll the ball in the bowl of icing sugar to coat it, then place it on the prepared tray. Repeat with the remaining mixture, ensuring the balls aren't too close together.

6 Gently press down each ball slightly using your index and middle finger. If using glacé cherries, place one in the centre of each biscuit, pressing it slightly into the dough. Dust the biscuits with a sprinkle of icing sugar, then bake for 12–15 minutes, checking at 12 minutes for doneness. The biscuits should be lightly golden and slightly cracked. Don't let them darken completely or they will over-cook and lose their signature texture.

7 Allow to cool completely on the tray so they set and become crisp.

MAMMA MARIA'S TIPS
- Be careful not to over-whisk the egg whites – if they're too stiff, they'll turn into meringue, which will affect the texture.
- Keep a bowl of water nearby when rolling the biscuits, to keep your hands from getting too sticky.
- Don't over-knead the dough – gentle mixing ensures a light texture.

INDEX

A
agrodolce 37
almond
   biscuits 219
   amaretti 227
amaretti biscotti 227
anchovies, fried dough balls 53
arancini
   filling 49
   Siciliani 49
arrabbiata pasta 145
arugula – see rocket
aubergine – see eggplant
authentic Neapolitan pizza 164–7

B
baked pasta 149
basil
   pesto 64
   and tomato sauce 60
   tomato and
     mozzarella salad 22
beans with pasta 141
béchamel sauce 67
beef
   Bolognese sauce 63
   bresaola salad 41
   saltimbocca 186
bell pepper, roasted 50
besciamella 67
biscotti
   amaretti 227
   di mandorla 219
biscuits, almond 219
Bolognese
   arancini 49
   sauce 63
braciole alla Calabrese 193
bread
   ciabatta 175
   focaccia 168
   fried mozzarella sandwiches 30
   no-knead loaf 171
   tomato bruschetta 26
breadcrumbs
   homemade 142
   with spaghetti 142
bresaola salad 41
broccoli and ricotta pasta 126
brodo della Nonna Igea 205
bruschetta di pomodoro 26
bucatini all'amatriciana 100

C
cacio e pepe 107
caggiunitt Abruzzesi 212
Calabrese
   salad 22
   stuffed meat rolls 193
calamari fritti 38
cannelloni
   filling 117
   **ricotta e spinaci della
     Nonna Igea 117**
cantucci 219
capers, pizza pockets 42
caponata Siciliana 37
capsicum, roasted 50
carbonara
   pasta 103
   with red sugo 100
cheese – see mozzarella, Parmigiano
   Reggiano, Pecorino Romano,
   ricotta
cheese balls 45
chicken
   cacciatore 198
   schnitzel 202
chilli and garlic pasta 154
chitarra alla Teramana 129–30
chitarra alla maccheroni 91
chitarra, use of 91
chocolate
   grape filling 212

    and ricotta crumble 224
    and ricotta filling 224
ciabatta bread 175
clams – *see* vongole
classic lasagna 121
coffee, tiramisù 215
conchiglioni ripieni al forno 112
cornmeal, polenta 150
cotoletta della Nonna Igea 202
courgette – *see* zucchini
cozze e vongole 206
crepes 114
crepes in broth from Teramo 205
crumble, ricotta and chocolate 224
custard, Italian-style 216

D
ditali pasta with beans 141
dressing, easy Italian 46

E
easy Italian dressing 46
egg pasta 80–3
egg
    carbonara pasta 103
    spinach frittata 54
eggplant
    parmigiana 190
    parmigiana spaghetti 146
    pasta 137
    salad 37
    stuffed 25

F
filling (savoury)
    arancini 49
    ricotta and spinach 112, 117
filling (sweet)
    chocolate grape 212
    ricotta and chocolate 224

fiori di zucca ripieni 34
fish
    fried 38
    fried dough balls with anchovies 53
focaccia Genovese 168
fresh egg pasta dough 80–3
fried
    arancini 49
    calamari 38
    cheese balls 45
    dough balls 53
mozzarella
    sandwiches 30
    pizza pockets 42
    pizza, Abruzzo style 178
    stuffed eggplants 25
    stuffed zucchini flowers 34
    sweet ravioli 212
frittata di spinaci 54
frittelle di zucchine 29
fritters, zucchini 29
fritto misto di mare 38

G
garlic
    bruschetta 26
    and chilli pasta 154
    marinara sauce 70
    roasted capsicums 50
gnocchi
    alla Sorrentina 157
    della Nonna Igea 95
    potato 95
    di ricotta 92
    with tomato and mozzarella 157
grape chocolate filling 212
grilled zucchini 46

H
hearty Italian soup 194

herbs – *see* basil, oregano
homemade
    breadcrumbs 142
    tomato passata 74

I
insalata
    Calabrese 22
    di bresaola 41
Italian dressing, easy 46
Italian meatballs 201
Italian-style custard 216

L
lamb shanks 197
lasagna
    classica 121
    traditional from Teramo 122–5
le polpette 201
le scrippelle 114
lemon
    limoncello 229
    pasta 158
limoncello della Nonna Igea 229
linguine alle vongole 111

M
maccheroni alla chitarra 91
Margherita pizza 172
marinara sauce 70
meatballs 201
meatballs, mini 129–30
melanzane
    alla parmigiana 90
    ripiene 25
minestrone 194
mini meatballs 129–30
mozzarella
    in carrozza 30
    sandwiches, fried 30

M (CONTINUED)
mozzarella (continued)
    tomato and basil salad 22
mushroom risotto 118
mussels and clams 206

N
Neapolitan sauce 70
no-knead
    artisan bread 171
    ciabatta bread loaves 175
    Neapolitan pizza dough 181
Nonna Igea's crepes 114
Nonna's broth 205
Nonna's schnitzel 202

O
oregano, marinara sauce 70
original spaghetti and meatballs from Teramo 129–30

P
pallotte cacio e ove 45
panna cotta 223
panzerotti Pugliesi 42
pappardelle
    handmade 80
    al ragù di cinghiale 138
    with wild boar sauce 138
parmigiana, eggplant 190
Parmigiano Reggiano
    basil pesto 64
    bresaola salad 41
passata rustica di pomodoro 74
passata, homemade 74
pasta
    al forno 149
    all'uovo 80–3
    alla gricia 108
    alla Norma 137
    ca muddica 142
    con broccoli e ricotta 126
    dough 80–3
    e fagioli di Nonna Igea 141
    preparation and storing 83
    verde agli spinaci 84
    see also Fresh Pasta 76–95, Primi 96–159
Pecorino cheese balls 45
penne all'arrabbiata 145
pepper – *see* capsicum, carbonara, chilli
pesto al basilico 64
pine nuts, basil pesto 64
pipi arrustuti 50
pizza dough
    authentic 164–7
    fried 53
    no-knead 181
pizza
    fried 178
    fritte della Nonna Igea 178
    Margherita 172
    Napoletana 164–7
pockets from Puglia 42
sauce 73
polenta al sugo con la salsiccia 150
polenta with tomato sauce and sausages 150
pollo alla cacciatora 198
polpettine 129–30
pomodori chini alla Calabrese 33
pomodori ripieni di Nonno Spataro 33
pork
    Bolognese sauce 63
    bucatini all'amatriciana 100
carbonara pasta 103
ribs with polenta 150
wild boar pasta 138
potato gnocchi 95
provolone and zucchini pasta 153

R
ragù alla Bolognese 63
ravioli
    della Nonna Igea 87–8
    fried sweet 212
    ricotta and spinach 87–8
rice – *see* arancini, risotto
ricotta
    and broccoli pasta 126
    and chocolate crumble 224
    and chocolate filling 224
    gnocchi 92
    and spinach cannelloni 117
    and spinach filling 112
    and spinach ravioli 87–8
    stuffed zucchini flowers 34
risotto
    al funghi 118
    alla Milanese 133
roasted capsicums 50
rocket, bresaola salad 41
Roman tripe 189

S
saffron risotto 133
salad
    bresaola 41
    Calabrese 22
    Sicilian eggplant 37
salsa di pomodoro per la pizza 73
saltimbocca 186
sandwiches, fried mozzarella 30
sauce (savoury)
    basil pesto 64
    béchamel 67
    Bolognese 63
    marinara 70
    pizza 73
    simple sugo 45
    tomato and basil 60
    see also Sauces 60–74

sauce (sweet)
    strawberry coulis 223
sausages with polenta 150
**sbriciolata alla ricotta
    e cioccolato 224**
**scrippelle 'mbusse della
    Nonna Igea 205**
seafood
    fried calamari 38
    linguine alle vongole 111
    mussels and clams 206
    pasta 104
Sicilian eggplant salad 37
simple sugo 45
slow-cooked lamb shanks 197
soup, minestrone 194
spaghetti
    aglio, olio e peperoncino 154
    al limone 158
    al pomodoro 134
    alla carbonara 103
    alla chitarra della Nonna Igea 91
    alla Nerano 153
    alla parmigiana 146
    alla scoglio 104
    with breadcrumbs 142
    with eggplant in
       tomato sauce 146
    and meatballs 129–30
    thick square 91
    with zucchini and provolone 153
spinach
    frittata 54
    pasta 84
    and ricotta cannelloni 117
    and ricotta filling 112
    and ricotta ravioli 87–8
stinco di agnello 197
strawberry coulis 223
stuffed
    eggplants 25
    pasta shells 112

rice balls 49
tomatoes 33
zucchini flowers 34
sugo
    alla marinara 70
    di pomodoro e basilico 60
    simple 45

T
tagliatelle, handmade 80–3
thick square spaghetti 91
**timballo alla Teramana
    di Nonna Igea 122–5**
tiramisù 215
tomato
    basil and mozzarella salad 22
    and basil sauce 60
    Bolognese sauce 63
    bruschetta 26
    and eggplant pasta 146
    marinara sauce 70
    and mozzarella gnocchi 157
    passata 74
    pasta 134
    pizza pockets 42
    sauce for pizza 73
    Sicilian eggplant salad 37
    simple sugo 45
    stuffed 33
    sugo 60, 45
traditional lasagna from
    Teramo 122–5
tripe 189
trippa alla Romana 189

V
veal
    cutlets with prosciutto
       and sage 186
    schnitzel 202

stuffed rolls 193
vongole
    linguine 111
    and mussels 206

W
white sauce, béchamel 67
wild boar pasta 138

Z
zabaglione 216
zeppole Calabrese 53
zucchine grigliate 46
zucchini
    flowers, stuffed 34
    fritters 29
    grilled 46
    and provolone pasta 153

For more recipes and to follow our journey,
visit: www.vincenzosplate.com

Join our authentic Italian foodie community via
www.youtube.com/vincenzosplate
@vincenzosplate

Sign up to our online course and
learn to master Italian cooking!
https://academy.vincenzosplate.com/

GRAZIE

A heartfelt thank you
To finally hold this book, after more than a decade of dreaming, cooking and storytelling, is a moment of profound joy. This journey is a testament to the power of food and family, navigating through both soaring highs and challenging lows.

The two lights that guided us
First, our incredible Vincenzo's Plate community. Your infectious passion, joy and unwavering love for authentic Italian food, culture and Vincenzo himself is the very oxygen of our purpose. You are our extended family, and we owe you everything for cheering us on daily.

Second, our unconditional love for our family and the legacy we build for our sons. Every page in this book is steeped in the hope that we can pass on the wisdom of the past – the meals that have stood the test of time – to enrich the next generation. This book is a love letter to Sebastian and Alessandro with a promise to always share the table.

The people who made it possible
To those who poured their talent, heart and spirit into these pages, your dedication is etched into the soul of this book:

Effi Tsoukatos, our extraordinary photographer: Thank you for taking a leap of faith, traveling to Italy and capturing the emotion and authenticity of our dishes. You didn't just take pictures; you used your craft to tell this story. Truly, grazie.

Cassie Gilmartin: The late nights, the endless video calls, the constant revisions – you are the unstoppable force who held the vision when ours sometimes wavered. You translated our dream into this reality, and for that we are eternally grateful.

Giota Letsios: Thank you for pouring your creativity into designing these pages and helping us craft this essential tool.

Lou Johnson: No one has been on this journey with us longer. From our first meeting to our SOS calls for advice from Italy, words don't cut it. Thank you for never doubting us.

Helen Littleton and the team at HarperCollins Australia: Your enthusiasm and belief in our book was integral to this project. Thank you for championing our story and giving it a home. Grazie mille.

The family and friends who stood by us
You are the quiet heroes who witnessed the heartache and the ultimate triumph behind every page. Thank you for standing by us and reminding us what truly matters. We are so lucky.

The soul of the recipes
And finally, to the magnificent individuals who feature in this book, particularly our beloved Nonna Igea. Your recipes are the soul of everything we do, and you are the ultimate example for our children.

We are so fortunate that you are always patient enough to share these treasures with us, even back when our community was just a distant dream. Nonna, we know you sometimes think we are crazy for wanting to film every step. Because of your patience and wisdom, so many people around the world have fallen in love with you.

Nonna, you remind countless people of their own nonnas, and thanks to you, your recipes and traditions will live on for generations.

HarperCollins_Publishers_
Australia • Brazil • Canada • France • Germany • Holland • India • Italy
Japan • Mexico • New Zealand • Poland • Spain • Sweden • Switzerland
United Kingdom • United States of America

HarperCollins acknowledges the Traditional Custodians of the lands upon which
we live and work, and pays respect to Elders past and present.

First published on Gadigal Country in Australia in 2026
by HarperCollins*Publishers* Australia Pty Limited
ABN 36 009 913 517
harpercollins.com.au

Copyright © Vincenzo and Suzanne Prosperi 2026

The right of Vincenzo and Suzanne Prosperi to be identified as the authors of this work has
been asserted by them in accordance with the *Copyright Act 1968*.

All rights reserved. Apart from any use as permitted under the *Copyright Act 1968*, no part
may be reproduced, copied, scanned, stored in a retrieval system, recorded, or transmitted, in
any form or by any means, without the prior written permission of the publisher. Without
limiting the exclusive rights of any author, contributor, or the publisher of this publication, any
unauthorised use of this publication to train generative artificial intelligence (AI) technologies
is expressly prohibited. HarperCollins also exercises its rights under Article 4(3) of the Digital
Single Market Directive 2019/790 and expressly reserves this publication from the text and
data-mining exception.

HarperCollins*Publishers*
Macken House, 39/40 Mayor Street Upper
Dublin 1, D01 C9W8, Ireland

A catalogue record for this book is available from the National Library of Australia

ISBN 978 1 4607 6910 2 (paperback)
ISBN 978 1 4607 1956 5 (ebook)

Publisher: Helen Littleton
Project editors: Shannon Kelly and Cassie Gilmartin
Copyeditor: Alex McDivitt
Cover and internal design by Giota Letsios
Cover and internal photography by Effi Tsoukatos
Index by Shannon Kelly
Colour reproduction by Splitting Image Colour Studio, Wantirna, Victoria
Printed and bound in China

8 7 6 5 4 3 2 1   26 27 28 29 30